Thank You 1095
Take the Thank You Challenge

by

Connie Ruth Christiansen

Bud Books
P.O. Box 822153
Vancouver, WA 98682

Thank You 1095 – Take the Thank You Challenge
ISBN-13: 978-0615573236
Copyright© 2011 by
Connie Ruth Christiansen
Bud Books
P.O. Box 822153
Vancouver, WA 98682

1st Printing; Printed in the United States of America. All rights reserved under International Copyright Law. Original contents may not be reproduced without the express written consent of the Publisher.

All quotations not original to this author are documented as such and credit is given to the original author.

Unless otherwise noted, all Scripture quotations are taken from the King James Version.

Scriptures marked NIV are taken from the Holy Bible, New International Version®, Copyright © 1973, 1978, 1984, 2011 by Biblica, Inc.™ Used by permission of Zondervan. All rights reserved worldwide. www.zondervan.com.

Scripture quotations marked NASB are taken from the New American Standard Bible® Copyright © 1960, 1962, 1963, 1968, 1971, 1972, 1973, 1975, 1977, 1995 by The Lockman Foundation Used by permission. www.Lockman.org.

Scripture quotations marked (NLT) are taken from the Holy Bible, New Living Translation, copyright © 1996, 2004, 2007 by Tyndale House Foundation. Used by permission of Tyndale House Publishers, Inc., Carol Stream, Illinois 60188. All rights reserved.

Scripture quotations marked "NKJV™" are taken from the New King James Version®. Copyright © 1982 by Thomas Nelson, Inc. Used by permission. All rights reserved.

Thank You 1095
Take the Thank You Challenge!

The Challenge:

Every Day for One Year:

1) Read a Short Inspirational.

2) Record 3 new things you are thankful for, in the space provided on each page.

After 365 days, look back at a list of 1,095 reasons to be grateful!

It's Easy

It's Fun

It Will Change Your Life!

For My
Beautiful Tanya.
I am
Thankful For You!

Thank You 1095
January 1

"There are only two ways to live your life. One is as though nothing is a miracle. The other is as if everything is a miracle."
~ *Albert Einstein, Physicist, Philosopher, Winner of the Nobel Prize, 1879-1936*

"Reflect upon your present blessings, of which every man has many; not on your past misfortunes, of which all men have some."
~ *Charles Dickens, Victorian English Author of Great Expectations, Oliver Twist, and A Christmas Carol, 1812-1870*

Thank You for:

1. _____

2. _____

3. _____

Thank You 1095
January 2

"Life is huge! Rejoice about the sun, moon, clouds, and sky, the flowers, grass and trees. Rejoice about the food you have to eat, the water you have to drink and swim in. Rejoice about the body that houses your spirit and the mind you have to learn and explore mysteries of life. Rejoice about the fact that you can be a positive force in the world around you. Rejoice about the love that is in you and surrounds you.
 If you want a happy full life, commit to making your life one of thankful rejoicing."
~ *Author Unknown*

"The most important prayer in the world is just two words long: "Thank You!""
~ *Meister Eckhart, German Theologian, Philosopher, Mystic, 1260-1327*

Thank You for:

 4. _____

 5. _____

 6. _____

Thank You 1095
January 3

"If the stars should appear but one night every thousand years, how man would marvel and stare."
~ *Ralph Waldo Emerson, American Philosopher, Poet, 1808-1882*

"If I were to be thankful for only the skies, that would be enough to live a grateful life until the day I die. Billions of stars, the planets, the moon, the black, the blue; the clouds changing shape, fluffy and soft, then heavy and grey; the sun shines from behind silver white rays too bright for my eyes, just right for my soul; and there on the horizon, between night and day are the colors of fire -- who cannot remain grateful in a sunset."
~ *Connie Ruth Christiansen*

Thank You for:

7. _____

8. _____

9. _____

Thank You 1095
January 4

"Consider how the lilies grow. They do not labor or spin. Yet I tell you, not even Solomon, in all of his splendor, was dressed like one of these."
~ *Luke 12:27 NIV*

"Every flower of the field, every fiber of a plant, every particle of an insect, carries with it the impress of its Maker, and can if duly considered read us lectures of ethics or divinity."
~ *Thomas Blount, American Revolutionary War Veteran, Statesman, 1486-1546*

"The temple bell stops but I hear the sound coming out of the flowers."
~ *Matsuo Basho, Japanese Poet, 1644-1694*

Thank You for:

10. _____

11. _____

12. _____

Thank You 1095
January 5

"Consider the ant."
~ *Proverbs 6:6a KJV*

"Even the creepy crawly things of earth are of infinite worth. Maybe you don't like to touch them maybe you do, but at least from afar, watch what they do. Spiders and beetles, caterpillars and worms, the tiniest of creatures we often ignore. Consider their comings and goings and learn. They speak to us of God."
~ *Connie Ruth Christiansen*

"I never could have thought of it, to have a little bug all lit, and made to go on wings."
~ *Elizabeth Maddox Roberts, American Novelist, Poet, 1881-1941*

Thank You for:

13. _____

14. _____

15. _____

Thank You 1095
January 6

"A truly happy person is one who can enjoy the scenery while on a detour."
~ *Author Unknown*

"In your busy day, going here and going there, doing this and doing that, determine to be aware of the things around you; that which has nothing to do with your prime objective. Give thanks for that thing you have noticed, and for the next thing that comes to mind, and then the next, and the next.

For instance, look up and see the birds on a wire and say: "Thank You for the birds, thank You for wires, thank You for telephone wires, for telephones, for communication, for talking, for people, for friends..."

As one idea triggers another has your journey been hindered? No. Has thanksgiving lifted your mind and heart and mood to a better place? Yes!"
~ *Connie Ruth Christiansen*

Thank You for:

16. _____

17. _____

18. _____

Thank You 1095
January 7

Think of random things to be thankful for:

"To poke a wood fire is more solid enjoyment than almost anything else in the world."
~ *Charles Dudley Warner, American Novelist, Co-writer with Mark Twain, 1829-1900*

"Nothing compares to the simple pleasure of a bike ride."
~ *John F. Kennedy, 35th U.S. President, 1917-1963*

"Never miss an opportunity to sleep on a screened porch."
~ *Ralph Waldo Emerson, American Philosopher, Poet, 1808-1882*

"It's fun having lots to do, but not doing it."
~ *Andrew Jackson, 7th U.S. President, 1767-1845*

Thank You for:

19. _____

20. _____

21. _____

Thank You 1095
January 8

"I wonder how many of us miss happy moments, not because we have none, but because we don't take the time to stop and enjoy them."
~ *Connie Ruth Christiansen*

"For each new morning with its light, for rest and shelter of the night; For health and food, for love and friends, for everything Thy goodness sends; For flowers that bloom about our feet, for tender grass, so fresh, so sweet; For song of bird, and hum of bee, for all things fair we hear or see; Father in heaven, we thank Thee!"
~ *Ralph Waldo Emerson, American Philosopher, Poet, 1808-1882*

Thank You for:

22. _____

23. _____

24. _____

Thank You 1095
January 9

"I love preliminary things; the tuning up of flutes and strings; The little scales musicians play, in varying keys to feel their way; The hum, the hush in which it dies, but most to see the curtain rise.

I love preliminary things, the little box the postman brings; To cut the twine, to break the seals, and wonder what the lid reveals; To lift the folds in which it lies, and watch the gift materialize.

The snowdrop and the daffodil, the catkins hanging straight and still; The blossom on the orchard trees, do you know greater joy than these? Each represents the hope that springs in all preliminary things."
~ Anticipation by J.R.J., Sunday Times, 1922

Thank You for:

25. _____

26. _____

27. _____

Thank You 1095
January 10

"Man is fond of counting his troubles, but he does not count his joys. If he counted them up as he ought to, he would see that every lot has enough happiness provided for it."
~ *Fyodor Dostoevsky, Russian Writer, Author of Crime and Punishment, 1821-1881*

"When I look at ugliness, I see beauty. When I am far from home, I see old friends. When there is noise, I hear a robin's song instead. When I am in a crowd, it is the mountain's peace I feel. In the winter of my sorrow, I remember the summer of my joy. In the nighttime of my loneliness, I breathe the day of my thanksgiving. But when the sadness spreads its blanket and that is what I see, I take my eyes to some high place until I find a reflection of what lies deep inside of me."
~ *Ancient Navajo Proverb*

Thank You for:

28. _____

29. _____

30. _____

Thank You 1095
January 11

"Remember God's bounty in the year. String the pearls of His favor. Hide the dark parts, except so far as they are breaking out in light! Give this one day to thanks, to joy, to gratitude."
~ *Henry Ward Beecher, Clergyman, Social Reformer, Abolitionist, 1813-1887*

"Remember and be thankful for all these: the success of perseverance; the pleasure of working; the dignity of simplicity; the worth of good character; the power of kindness; the influence of example; the obligation of duty; the wisdom of economy; the virtue of patience; the improvement of talent; the joy of originating."
~ *Author Unknown*

Thank You for:

31. _____

32. _____

33. _____

Thank You 1095
January 12

"I am thankful for God's love. It is my sustaining power through all things that were, all things that are, and all things that will be. Without it I would be lost."
~ Carl (Bud) Christiansen, 87, Retired Preacher, Musician, Craftsperson, Stone Mason; Used by permission

"Where can I go from Your spirit? Where can I flee from Your presence? If I go up to the heavens, You are there; if I make my bed in the depths, You are there. If I rise on the wings of the dawn, if I settle on the far side of the sea, even there Your hand will guide me, Your right hand will hold me fast."
~ Psalm 139:6-10 NIV

Thank You for:

34. _____

35. _____

36. _____

Thank You 1095
January 13

"Deposit all the grateful happiness you can into your bank account of memories."
~ Author Unknown

"You are forever building a memory collage of things accomplished and things procrastinated; of things contented and things regretted. An embittered heart will result in bleak memories of both painful and joyful events. A thankful heart will arrange beauty into even the most difficult of situations.
 Do not weigh yourself down with the dreary of memories dark with ingratitude. Instead carry with you memories that are lightened and brightened by appreciation."
~ Connie Ruth Christiansen

Thank You for:

37. _____

38. _____

39. _____

Thank You 1095
January 14

"Time is full of eternity. As we use it so shall we be. Every day has its opportunities, every hour its offer of grace."
   ~ Henry Edward Manning, English Roman Catholic Archbishop, 1808-1892

"Choose to love rather than to hate, to smile rather than to frown. Choose to build rather than to destroy, to persevere rather than to quit. Choose to praise rather than to gossip, to heal rather than to wound. Choose to give rather than to grasp, to go rather than to delay. Choose to forgive rather than to curse, to pray rather than to despair. Choose to meditate on good rather than on evil, to cultivate thankfulness rather than to complain."
   ~ Author Unknown; A similar quotation has been attributed to Rod Woodson's 2009 acceptance speech into the Football Hall of Fame

Thank You for:

40. _____

41. _____

42. _____

Thank You 1095
January 15

"Attitude is a little thing that makes a big difference."
~ *Winston Churchill, British WWII Leader, Politician, Statesman, 1874-1965*

"Your living is determined not so much by what life brings to you as by the attitude you bring to life; not so much by what happens to you as by the way your mind looks at what happens."
~ *Khalil Gibran, Lebanese American Artist, Poet, Author of The Prophet, 1883-1931*

"Yank some of the groans out of your prayers, and shove in some shouts of thanksgiving."
~ *Billy Sunday, National League Baseball Player, Evangelist, 1862-1935*

Thank You for:

43. _____

44. _____

45. _____

Thank You 1095
January 16

"To everything there is a season, a time for every purpose under heaven.

There is a time to be born and a time to die, a time to laugh and a time to cry.

There is a time to reap and a time to sow, a time to tear and a time to sew.

There is a time to embrace and a time to refrain, a time to lose and a time to gain.

There is a time to break down and a time to enhance, a time to mourn and a time to dance.

There is a time to destroy and a time to heal, a time to speak and a time to be still.

There is a time of love and a time of hate, a time of war and a time of peace."
~ *Adapted from Proverbs 3: 1-8; Connie Ruth Christiansen*

Thank You for:

46. _____

47. _____

48. _____

Thank You 1095
January 17

"If I will accept the sunshine and warmth, then I must also accept the thunder and the lightning."
~ *Khalil Gibran, Lebanese American Poet, Author of The Prophet, 1883-1931*

"God has not promised skies always blue, flower-strewn pathways all our lives through; God has not promised sun without rain, joy without sorrow, peace without pain. But God has promised strength for the day, rest for the labor, light for the way, grace for the trials, help from above, unfailing sympathy, undying love."
~ *Annie Johnson Flint, child orphan, crippled as an adult, Poet, 1866-1932*

Thank You for:

49. _____

50. _____

51. _____

Thank You 1095
January 18

"There are glimpses of heaven to us in every act, or thought, or word, or song that raises us above ourselves."
~ *Robert Quillen, American Journalist, Humorist, Editor, Humanitarian, 1887-1848*

"Open my eyes, that I may see glimpses of truth *You have* for me; Place in my hands the wonderful key that shall unclasp and set me free. Open my ears, that I may hear voices of truth *You send* clear; And while the wave notes fall on my ear, everything false will disappear."
~ *Hymn by Clara H. Scott, Musician, Teacher, Author, 1841-1897*

Thank You for:

52. _____

53. _____

54. _____

Thank You 1095
January 19

"They that wait upon the Lord shall renew their strength, they shall mount up with wings as eagles, they shall run and not be weary, they shall walk and not faint."
~ *Isaiah 40:31 KJV*

"Thank You for the valleys, and the waiting times. For in those lonely hours Your comfort has been mine.
Thank You for the baby steps, and for when I fall. For it is when I'm small and weak I need You most of all.
Thank You for the mountains I am forced to climb. For on those rocky cliffs I have grown my wings to fly."
~ *Connie Ruth Christiansen*

Thank You for:

55. _____

56. _____

57. _____

Thank You 1095
January 20

"Moments come and moments go, celebrate them as they fly by; you cannot get them back.

Seasons come and seasons go, revel in the wind, the sun, the rain; no day will ever be the same.

People come and people go, cling to what you can of them; there will be a time when they will not come again."
~ Connie Ruth Christiansen

"This moment contains all moments."
~ C. S. Lewis, British Teacher, Author, Theologian
1898-1963

Thank You for:

58. _____

59. _____

60. _____

Thank You 1095
January 21

"When eating bamboo sprouts, remember the man who planted them."
~ *Ancient Chinese Proverb*

"Take the time to recall, and be thankful for the many people who make the conveniences of your life possible: The gas station attendant and the grocery clerk, the farmer, the gardener, the rancher, and the ones that collect the eggs from under the chickens, the fire fighter, the police officer, the doctor, and the nurse, the shipping and handling clerk, the bus driver, the street sweeper, the mail carrier, the newspaper deliverer, the news reporter, the weather reporter, the TV repair person, the plumber, the carpenter, the bridge builders, the computer geniuses that formatted your favorite website; the list goes on."
~ *Connie Ruth Christiansen*

Thank You for:

61. _____

62. _____

63. _____

Thank You 1095
January 22

"A story is told of a woman who was always joyful, and always had a thank you on her lips. When asked her secret, she answered that she had learned a thankful heart from her father:

"My family was large and terribly poor, but still we often shared everything we had with our friends and neighbors. Whenever we were down to our last five dollars, my father would say: "Let's have a party!" He would then spend that five dollars on treats such as ice cream, and invite all the neighbors to come over. In spite of that, or perhaps because of that, we always had everything we needed.""
~ *Author Unknown*

"When you have only two pennies left in the world, buy a loaf of bread with one, and a lily with the other."
~ *Ancient Chinese Proverb*

Thank You for:

64. _____

65. _____

66. _____

Thank You 1095
January 23

"The best things are nearest: breath in your nostrils, light in your eyes, flowers at your feet, duties at your hand, the path of God before you."
~ Robert Louis Stevenson, Scottish Author of Dr. Jekyll & Mr. Hyde, and Treasure Island, 1850-1894

"To find the air and the water exhilarating; to be refreshed by a morning walk or an evening saunter, to be thrilled by the stars at night, to be elated over a bird's nest or a wildflower in the spring – these are rewards of the simple life."
~ John Burroughs, American Philosopher, Naturalist, Writer, 1837-1921

"Rejoice in the things that are present."
~ Michel de Montaigne, French Renaissance Writer, 1533-1592

Thank You for:

67. _____

68. _____

69. _____

Thank You 1095
January 24

"One day a little boy was playing in his front yard when he noticed his neighbor (whose wife had recently died) crying. Putting aside his toy truck, the youngster hoisted himself over the dividing fence, walked over to his grey-haired friend and climbed up onto his lap. He stayed there for quite some time, then gave the man a hug, hopped down and back over the fence to resume his play.

Later that evening the boy's mother asked what the two of them had talked about. "Nothin'," the child replied. "I was just helpin' him cry.""
~ *Author Unknown*

"From the lips of children and infants you have ordained praise (strength)."
~ *Matthew 21:16; Psalm 8:2 NIV*

Thank You for:

70. _____

71. _____

72. _____

Thank You 1095
January 25

"Confess your faults to one another, and pray for one another so that you may be healed."
~ James 5:16 NASB

"I am thankful that healing has been provided us through a variety of avenues: prayer, faith, friendship, exercise, rest, heat, cold, time, touch, massage, pressure, elevation, traction, radiation, food, medicine, surgery, hope, laughter, miracles; all of which have been given us by our Creator. And when death finds us, ultimate healing will be ours in that other Realm where there is no more sickness, no more sadness, no more pain."
~ Connie Ruth Christiansen

Thank You for:

73. _____

74. _____

75. _____

Thank You 1095
January 26

"In Your presence is fullness of joy."
~ Psalm 16:11 NKJV

"In my spirit, which understands that which my mind cannot comprehend, I know that You are always near. But oh how I long for; live for those transitory moments when my faith becomes sight, when my natural and spirit eyes are one, heaven and earth merge within me, around me, the incredible sense of Love's otherworld is all-consuming, lifts me away from earth's heaviness, swallows up all of my fears and answers all of my questions, just enough to make me homesick for my journey's end, just enough to give me strength to pick back up some heavy of this earth, lighter now somehow, just enough for joy to journey onward."
~ Connie Ruth Christiansen

Thank You for:

76. _____

77. _____

78. _____

Thank You 1095
January 27

"I had the blues because I had no shoes until upon the street I met a man who had no feet."
~ Ancient Persian Saying

"There may not be much money, friends may let you down, disappointment everywhere around. Still, there's so much to be thankful for.

For every breath we breathe, every step we take, every decision that we freely make; For the baby in the crib, the puppy in the yard, the mountains rivers flowers, sun moon and stars; For the beauty that surrounds even our fears; For laughter, for tears, for our time here; Thank You."
~ Adapted from For This Life, song by Connie Ruth Christiansen

Thank You for:

79. _____

80. _____

81. _____

Thank You 1095
January 28

"You may say "It's impossible."
God says "All things are possible."
~ Luke 18:27
You may say "I can't go on."
God says "My grace is sufficient."
~ Corinthians 12:9
You may say "I don't know what to do, what to say, or where to go."
God says "I will direct your steps."
~ Proverbs 3:5-6
You may say "I'm not smart enough."
God says "I will give you wisdom."
~ I Corinthians 1:30
You may way "I don't have enough."
God says "I will supply all your need."
~ Philippians 4:19"
~ Author Unknown

Thank You for:

82. _____

83. _____

84. _____

Thank You 1095
January 29

"The Lord is my shepherd; I shall not want. He makes me to lie down in green pastures; He leads me beside the still waters; He restores my soul; He leads me in the paths of righteousness for His name's sake. Yea, though I walk through the valley of the shadow of death, I will fear no evil, for You are with me; Your rod and Your staff, they comfort me. You prepare a table before me in the presence of my enemies; You anoint my head with oil; My cup runs over."
~ Psalm 23: 1-5 NKJV

"Be thankful that the closer we walk to the Shepherd, the farther we are from the wolf."
~ Author Unknown

Thank You for:

85. _____

86. _____

87. _____

Thank You 1095
January 30

"To say "thank you" takes only a moment, but has the potential to change an hour, a day, a lifetime."
~ *Connie Ruth Christiansen*

"Let us rise up and be thankful, for if we didn't learn a lot today, at least we learned a little, and if we didn't learn a little, at least we didn't get sick, and if we got sick, at least we didn't die; so, let us all be thankful."
~ *Ancient Chinese Proverb*

"God gave you a gift of 86,400 seconds today. Have you used one to say thank You?"
~ *William A. Ward, one of America's most quoted writers of inspirational maxims, 1921-1994*

Thank You for:

88. _____

89. _____

90. _____

Thank You 1095
January 31

"Do not neglect to show hospitality to strangers, for by this some have entertained angels without knowing it."
~ *Hebrews 13:1 NASB*

"At any given moment the events of our days are so much more than we can see, hear, or feel with our natural senses. There is a spiritual world busy all around us, beneath us, above us. He sends His heavenly messengers to earth. We may or may not see them; we may or may not choose to appreciate them. They continue as our devotees, with or without our gratefulness."
~ *Connie Ruth Christiansen*

Thank You for:

91. _____

92. _____

93. _____

Thank You 1095
February 1

"The best and most beautiful things in this world cannot be seen or even heard, but must be felt with the heart."
~ Helen Keller, American Author, Political Activist, Lecturer, blind and deaf from childhood, 1880-1968

"The pain and the sorrow are part of the joy; the loss is part of the gain. The dying is part of the living. Beauty will both break and heal the heart."
~ Connie Ruth Christiansen

Thank You for:

94. _____

95. _____

96. _____

Thank You 1095
February 2

"A group of young students were asked to list what they thought were the present Seven Wonders of the World. For most, their list was similar to that in the history books: Egypt's Great Pyramids, Grand Canyon, Panama Canal, Empire State Building, St. Peter's Basilica, China's Great Wall.

The teacher noticed that one quiet student hadn't turned in a paper yet, so she asked the girl if she was having trouble with the list. The child hesitated, and then shyly read: "I think the Seven Wonders of the World are: To touch, To taste, To see, To hear, To feel, To laugh, To love."

A silent reverence filled the room at the realization that the things we often take for granted, are truly the most wondrous."
~ Author Unknown

Thank You for:

97. _____

98. _____

99. _____

Thank You 1095
February 3

"Trouble knocked on the door, but, hearing laughter, hurried away."
~ *Benjamin Franklin, U. S. Founding Father, Civic Activist, Statesman, Diplomat, Inventor, 1706-1790*

"Guffaws and giggles, chortles and snorts, rat-a-tat-tats and big loud blats, gentle and quiet, with tears or without, boisterous the kind that is almost a shout, the just passing by for a moment kind that leaves a willing smile behind, the lingers for a long time, builds up from deep within comes up from the toes and spills up and over and out contagious kind, the makes you sit up and listen kind, the lasts so long it actually hurts and doubles you physically over kind, the forces you to respond kind, even when you are determined not to smile, you must smile. Thank You for all the many sounds and sights of laughter."
~ *Connie Ruth Christiansen*

Thank You for:

100. _____

101. _____

102. _____

Thank You 1095
February 4

"For God has not given us the spirit of fear; but of power, and of love, and of a sound mind."
~ *2 Timothy 1:7 NKJV*

"Think of the wild erratic beating of your heart as your inner applause. "Good job!" Your heart is crying out. "Don't stop now! You can do this!" Think of your shortness of breath as that of a runner who has come such a long way, and is just about to cross the finish line.

All the voices in your head, the negative ones that have been telling you to stop trying are changing their tune as they see you coming around the bend. The crowd jumps to their feet, roaring with excitement. It is not fear you sense within; it is your standing ovation!"
~ *Connie Ruth Christiansen*

Thank You for:

103. _____

104. _____

105. _____

Thank You 1095
February 5

"Guidelines for a happy life: Free your heart from hate; Be thankful for what you can do; Let go of what you can't do; Free your mind from worry; Fill your mind with joyful thoughts; Live simple; Give more; Expect less."
~ *Author Unknown*

"Make the most of yourself, for that is all there is of you."
~ *Ralph Waldo Emerson, American Philosopher, Poet, 1808-1882*

"And in the end, it's not the years in your life that count. It's the life in your years."
~ *Abraham Lincoln, 16th President of the U.S., 1809-1865*

Thank You for:

106. _____

107. _____

108. _____

Thank You 1095
February 6

"I have learned silence from the talkative, toleration from the intolerant, and kindness from the unkind."
   ~ Khalil Gibran, Lebanese American Artist, Poet, Author of The Prophet, 1883-1931

"Every person in your life whether nemesis or proponent, brings some sense of meaning and worth. If nothing else they challenge you to be a better you. Be thankful for that."
   ~ Connie Ruth Christiansen

"Some people weave burlap into the fabric of our lives, and some weave goldthread. Both contribute to make the whole picture beautiful and unique."
   ~ Author Unknown

Thank You for:

   109. _____

   110. _____

   111. _____

Thank You 1095
February 7

"Your heart knows in silence the secrets of the days and nights, but your ears thirst for the sound of your heart's knowledge."
~ *Khalil Gibran, Lebanese American Artist, Poet, Author of The Prophet, 1883-1931*

"Death and life are in the power of the tongue, and those who love it will eat its fruit."
~ *Proverbs 18:21 NKJV*

"Thank You on the tongue is music to the ears; music to the ears is light for the soul; light for the soul is strength of life."
~ *Connie Ruth Christiansen*

Thank You for:

112. _____

113. _____

114. _____

Thank You 1095
February 8

"I love things that go snap and crackle, tap and pop; corn dancing on the fire, and cereal that talks to milk; bubble gum and fire crackers and snapping my fingers in time to the music; toast popping up from the toaster, warm and just the right shade of brown; eyes popping open in excitement or delight; hands popping up around the room in answer to a teacher's question; the crackle of a fire and the snap of a suspender; the popping of a sore neck and the crackle of tired knuckles; tapping rain on the window, tap shoes on the floor; a tap at the door announcing an arrival...Thank You for all of the many snaps and crackles, taps and pops."
~ *Connie Ruth Christiansen*

"In everything give thanks."
~ *I Thessalonians 5:8 KJV*

Thank You for:

115. _____

116. _____

117. _____

Thank You 1095
February 9

"If you want to feel rich, just count the things you have that money can't buy."
~ *Author Unknown*

"The materials of wealth are in the earth, in the seas, and in their natural and unaided productions."
~ *Daniel Webster, American Statesman, Senator, 1782-1852*

"God hides things by putting them all around us."
~ *Author Unknown*

Thank You for:

118. _____

119. _____

120. _____

Thank You 1095
February 10

"As a single footstep will not make a path on the earth, so a single thought will not make a pathway in the mind. To make a deep physical path, we walk again and again. To make a deep mental path, we must think over and over the kind of thoughts we wish to dominate our lives."
~ *Henry David Thoreau, Author, Poet, Naturalist, Abolitionist, Philosopher, 1817-1862*

"I can no other answer make, but thanks, and thanks, and thanks."
~ *William Shakespeare, English Poet, Playwright, 1564- 1616*

Thank You for:

121. _____

122. _____

123. _____

Thank You 1095
February 11

"How far that little candle throws his beams! So shines a good deed in a weary world."
~ William Shakespeare, English Poet, Playwright, 1564- 1616

"For the genteel old man whose gnarled hands held open the door to let me pass first, the teenage boy who offered his seat on the bus, the little child who giggled at a wink, the stranger passing by who took the time to smile, for all the kindnesses ever shown me everywhere, anytime, any day, thank You."
~ Connie Ruth Christiansen

Thank You for:

124. --

125. --

126. --

Thank You 1095
February 12

"Do not regret growing older. It's a privilege denied to some."
~ *Author Unknown*

"Even as we age, there is still a lot to be thankful for, if you take the time to look. For example, I'm sitting here thinking how nice it is that wrinkles don't hurt."
~ *Author Unknown*

"How beautiful the leaves grow old. How full of light and color are their last days."
~ *John Burroughs, American Philosopher, Naturalist, Writer, 1837-1921*

Thank You for:

127. _____

128. _____

129. _____

Thank You 1095
February 13

"How many times do we miss God's blessings because they are not packaged as we expected?"
~ Author Unknown

"*He* was showered with kindly care at the farmer's house. In this way, the *lonely* ugly duckling was able to survive the bitterly cold winter. *In the* springtime the duckling saw himself mirrored in the water. "Goodness! How I've changed! I hardly recognize myself!" Now, he swam majestically with his fellow swans. One day, he heard children on the river bank exclaim: "Look at that young swan! He's the finest of them all!" And he almost burst with happiness."
~ Adapted from The Ugly Duckling by Hans Christian Anderson, 1805-1875

Thank You for:

130. _____

131. _____

132. _____

Thank You 1095
February 14

"I praise You because I am fearfully and wonderfully made; Your works are wonderful, I know that full well."
~ *Psalm 139:19 NIV*

"People travel to wonder at the height of the mountains, at the huge waves of the seas, at the long course of the rivers, at the vast compass of the ocean, at the circular motion of the stars, and yet they pass by themselves without wondering."
~ *St. Augustine, Early Century Christian Priest, Author, 354-430*

"Always act like you are wearing an invisible crown."
~ *Author Unknown*

Thank You for:

133. _____

134. _____

135. _____

Thank You 1095
February 15

"When it seems you can think of nothing more to be thankful for; you want to be thankful, but what is left to add to the list? Just look around the room. Do you have a table or a chair, a stereo, a TV, a mirror, a desk, a computer, a waste basket, a dresser, a book, a lampshade, a closet, clothes, pictures on the wall, paint on the wall? We are inundated with blessing.

How many times a day do we pick up a pen, a cup, a fork, a knife; turn on a light, a radio, a heater; climb onto a bed, a chair, a ladder; feel bare floors or carpet beneath our toes; and never stop to consider the blessing of each, never wonder what life would be like without them; never say "Thank You.""
~ *Connie Ruth Christiansen*

Thank You for:

136. _____

137. _____

138. _____

Thank You 1095
February 16

"I think that some people will grumble at even the accommodations of Heaven. How different the thankful heart.

What a gift it is to be born with an outlook toward the bright side of things. And if not so by nature, what a triumph of grace to be made thankful through a renewed heart! It is so much more comfortable and rational to see what we have to be thankful for, and to rejoice accordingly, than to have our vision forever filled with our lacks and our needs. Happy are they who possess the gift of thanksgiving!"
~ *Author Unknown*

"There is always, always, always something to be thankful for."
~ *Author Unknown*

Thank You for:

139. _____

140. _____

141. _____

Thank You 1095
February 17

"We would worry less if we praised more. Thanksgiving is the enemy of discontent."
~ *Henry A. Ironside, Canadian Teacher, Pastor, Author, 1876-1951*

"Deliver us from the fretfulness of self-pitying; make us sure of the good we cannot see, of the hidden good in the world."
~ *Eleanor Roosevelt, First Lady of the U.S., 1884-1962*

"If things are going well, enjoy it because it won't last forever. If things are going bad, don't worry because it won't last forever either."
~ *Author Unknown*

Thank You for:

142. _____

143. _____

144. _____

Thank You 1095
February 18

"Hope is the thing with feathers that perches in the soul; and sings the tune without the words, and never stops—at all. And sweetest in the Gale is heard, and sore must be the storm; that could abash the little Bird that kept so many warm."
~ *Emily Dickinson, American Poet, 1830-1886*

"Thank You for the light at the end of the tunnel, the bend ahead in the road, the finish line, the journey's end, a new day after a restless night, joy after tears."
~ *Connie Ruth Christiansen*

Thank You for:

145. _____

146. _____

147. _____

Thank You 1095
February 19

"God has chosen the foolish things of the world to shame the wise, and God has chosen the weak things of the world to shame the things which are strong."
~ *Corinthians 1:27 NASB*

"The most physically strong man in the world will never be more powerful than the grasp of a newborn baby's tiny hand. The arrogance of a brilliant scientific scholar is humbled by the trusting innocence of a child's question, "why?""
~ *Connie Ruth Christiansen*

Thank You for:

148. _____

149. _____

150. _____

Thank You 1095
February 20

"Living thankful doesn't mean that you think everything is perfect. It means that you've decided to look beyond the imperfections."
~ *Author Unknown*

"Three people were at work on the same construction site. When each was asked what the job was, the answers varied: "Breaking rocks," replied the first. "Earning my living," the second answered. "Building a cathedral," said the third."
~ *Author Unknown*

"My great-grandfather was President of the United States, my grandfather was Senator of Ohio, my father is Ambassador to Ireland, and *I* am a Brownie."
~ *Attributed to the young daughter of William Howard Taft, III*

Thank You for:

151. _____

152. _____

153. _____

Thank You 1095
February 21

"The six most important words: I admit I made a mistake. The five most important words: You did a good job. The four most important words: What is YOUR opinion? The three most important words: If you please. The two most important words: Thank You. The one most important word: We. The least important word: I."
~ *Author Unknown*

"We can only be said to be alive in those moments when our hearts are conscious of our treasures."
~*Thornton Wilder, American Playwright, Novelist, Pulitzer Prize winner, 1897-1995*

Thank You for:

154. _____

155. _____

156. _____

Thank You 1095
February 22

"If you woke up this morning with more health than illness, you are more blessed than the million who will not survive the week.

If you have food in your refrigerator, clothes on your back, a roof over your head and a place to sleep, you are richer than 75 percent of the world.

If you have money in the bank or in your wallet, you are among the top 80 percent of the worlds' wealthy.

If you hold up your head with a smile on your face and are truly thankful, you are blessed because the majority can, but many do not."
~ *Author Unknown*

"Thank You, dear God for all you have given me, for all you have taken away from me, for all you have left me."
~ *Author Unknown*

Thank You for:

157. _____

158. _____

159. _____

Thank You 1095
February 23

"I know this world is ruled by infinite intelligence. Everything that surrounds us, everything that exists proves that there are infinite laws behind it. There can be no denying this fact. It is mathematical in its precision."
~ *Thomas Edison, Businessman, Scientist, Inventor*
1847-1941

"Thomas Edison studied the mathematical, electrical, and other mysteries of life, and he recognized the Source from which those mysteries come. He found ways to create from his discoveries and produced more than 1,000 inventions in his lifetime.
Be thankful that there are still mysteries to uncover, and still more to learn about the God who delights in our discovering His hidden treasures. And be thankful that there is vision within us to turn those discoveries into unique treasures that potentially will contain mysteries of their own for others to explore."
~ *Connie Ruth Christiansen*

Thank You for:

160. _____

161. _____

162. _____

Thank You 1095
February 24

"Just in time for dinner, some neighborhood children wandered in, as they often do. While we shared a meal, I popped an old 80's record on the turntable. They were mesmerized, watching it go round and round. When the tunes were over and their bellies full, they said their goodbyes.

The next evening I answered a knock at the door to find some unfamiliar children, who had never visited us before. They asked if they could please come in and listen to the "giant CD player."

The news had spread quickly regarding this electronic wonder. These children, who have not known a world without computers, DVDs and iPods, had never before seen a record player.

How fast our world changes. Be thankful for the many new blessings each generation creates and experiences. Be thankful for the memories unique to your own generation."
~ *Connie Ruth Christiansen*

Thank You for:

163. _____

164. _____

165. _____

Thank You 1095
February 25

"During Thomas Jefferson's presidency, he and a group of his men came to a river that had overflowed its banks. One by one each man began to cross over the treacherous waters on horseback; fighting for his life. A lone traveler on foot stood watching the group, and then finally asked Mr. Jefferson to take him across. The President agreed without hesitation, and so the man climbed on to the back of his horse. The horse carried the two men to safety.

On the other side, someone asked the man, "Why did you select the President to ask for a ride?" The man was shocked, admitting he had no idea he had approached the President of the United States. "All I know," he said, "is that on some of your faces was written the answer *No* and on some of them was the answer *Yes*. His was a *Yes* face."

Be thankful for the *Yes* faces of your life."
~ *Author Unknown*

Thank You for:

166. _____

167. _____

168. _____

Thank You 1095
February 26

"What I am wishing for my beautiful grandchildren: I hope that you wear hand-me-down clothes, eat homemade ice cream, and leftover meatloaf sandwiches; Skin your knees climbing a tree, and stick your tongue to a frozen flagpole; Learn humility by being humiliated, and honesty by being cheated; Make your own bed, mow the lawn, and wash the car; Share a bedroom with your younger sibling, and let them climb under the covers with you when they're scared; Walk uphill to school with your friends, and that you live in a town where it is safe to do so; Learn to make a slingshot instead of buying one and learn to add and subtract in your head; Dig in the dirt, and read books; Sit on a porch with your grandparents, go shopping with your aunt, and fishing with your uncle; Learn to appreciate tough times, hard work disappointments, and happiness; Appreciate your life."
~ *Author Unknown*

Thank You for:

169. _____

170. _____

171. _____

Thank You 1095
February 27

"Abraham Lincoln
Failed in business in 1831
Defeated for Legislature in 1832
Second failure in business in 1833
Suffered a nervous breakdown in 1836
Defeated for Speaker of the House in 1838
Defeated for Elector in 1840
Defeated for Congress in 1843
Defeated for Senate in 1855
Defeated for Vice President in 1856
Defeated for Senate in 1858
Elected President in 1860."
~ Author Unknown

"Success is going from failure to failure without losing enthusiasm."
~ Winston Churchill, British WWII Leader, Politician, Statesman, 1874-1965

Thank You for:

172. _____

173. _____

174. _____

Thank You 1095
February 28

"Ask and it will be given."
~ *Matthew 7:7 NKJV*

"I asked for strength and I was granted a weakness, so that I might feel the need for God. I prayed for wisdom and He gave me problems to solve. I asked for prosperity and I was given brain and brawn to work. I asked for courage and faced dangers to overcome. I asked for love and found troubled people who needed help. I asked for health that I might do greater things, I was allowed infirmity, that I might do better things. I asked for favors and God gave me opportunities.

I asked for all things that I might enjoy life, I was given life that I might enjoy all things. In the end I received nothing I wanted and everything I needed. I am among all men most richly blessed."
~ *Author Unknown*

Thank You for:

175. _____

176. _____

177. _____

Thank You 1095
March 1

"The unthankful heart discovers no mercies; but let the thankful heart sweep through the day and, as a magnet finds the iron, so it will find, in every hour, some heavenly blessings."
~ Henry Ward Beecher, Clergyman, Social Reformist, Abolitionist, Speaker, 1813-1887

"Where others see but the dawn coming over the hill, I see the soul of God shouting for joy."
~ William Blake, English Romantic Poet and Painter, 1757-1827

Thank You for:

178. _____

179. _____

180. _____

Thank You 1095
March 2

"A young woman planted a flower garden, but when the flowers came up so did a great crop of dandelions among them. She consulted with gardeners near and far, but none of their ideas worked. Finally, the young woman traveled to the palace to seek the wisdom of the royal gardener himself. But alas, she had already tried all the methods the kindly old man had to recommend. "Well then," the royal gardener said, "the only thing I can suggest is that you welcome these flowering weeds into your garden, enjoy their unique beauty, and be thankful for them.""
~ *Author Unknown*

"They whom truth and wisdom lead, can gather honey from a weed."
~ *William Cowper, English Poet, Hymnist, 1731-1800*

Thank You for:

181. _____

182. _____

183. _____

Thank You 1095
March 3

"To have a full stomach and fixed income are no small things."
    ~ Elbert Hubbard, American Writer, Publisher, Artist, Philosopher, 1856-1915

"I thank God for dirty dishes; they have a tale to tell. While other folks go hungry, we're eating pretty well. With home and health, and happiness, we shouldn't want to fuss; for by this stack of evidence, God's very good to us."
    ~ Author Unknown

"Gratitude unlocks the fullness of life. It turns what we have into enough, and more."
    ~ Author Unknown

Thank You for:

184. _____

185. _____

186. _____

Thank You 1095
March 4

"How precious are Your thoughts towards me, O God; how great is the sum of them."
~ *Psalm 139:17-18 NKJV*

"Thank You for giving me a mind to think, and ideas to explore; for moments of wisdom and moments of wonder; for thoughts beyond myself and for creative impulses and intuition; for questions, for finding answers, and for questions that have answers too big for me.

Thank You for the Mind that thought me into being, that surrounded me with miracles and with mysteries. Thank You that Your thoughts are far beyond my own, that You have all the answers; that You hold them in Your heart. And thank You that although I may never comprehend the total of Your mind, I can apprehend the essence of Your heart."
~ *Connie Ruth Christiansen*

Thank You for:

187. _____

188. _____

189. _____

Thank You 1095
March 5

"If you love the good that you see in another, you make it your own."
~ *Pope Gregory I, AKA Gregory the Great, 540-604*

"Be thankful that we can look to the success of others and follow their example toward success of our own."
~ *Author Unknown*

"He who walks with wise men will grow wise."
~ *Proverbs 13:20 NKJV*

Thank You for:

190. _____

191. _____

192. _____

Thank You 1095
March 6

"I am so fond of tea that I could write a whole dissertation on its virtues. It comforts and enlivens – a safe inspirer of social joy."
~ *James Boswell, Scottish Biographer, 1740-1795*

"A cup of coffee, real coffee, home-browned, home ground, home-made, that comes to you dark, but changes to golden bronze as you temper it with cream that is neither lumpy nor frothing on the Java; such a cup of coffee is a match for anything good."
~ *Henry Ward Beecher, American Minister, 1813-1887*

"Swallowing hot chocolate before it has cooled off takes you by surprise at first, but it keeps you warm and happy for a long time."
~ *Author Unknown*

Thank You for:

193. _____

194. _____

195. _____

Thank You 1095
March 7

"Life without thankfulness is devoid of love and passion.

Hope without thankfulness is lacking in fine perception.

Faith without thankfulness lacks strength and fortitude.

Every virtue divorced from thankfulness is maimed and limps along the spiritual road."
~ *John Henry Jowett, American Theologian, Pastor, 1864-1923*

"A thankful heart is not only the greatest virtue but the parent of all other virtues."
~ *Cicero, Roman Statesman, Lawyer, Philosopher, 106-43 BC*

Thank You for:

196. _____

197. _____

198. _____

Thank You 1095
March 8

"There is no color in this world that is not intended to make us rejoice."
~ *John Calvin, French Lawyer, Theologian, Founder of Calvinism, 1509-1564*

"For the color of flowers and the blue of sky, and for rainbows; for crayons and coloring books and pillows on a sofa; for red, yellow, pink, purple and orange; for color arrangements of beauty by You, and by the imagination of those You have created in Your own image, thank You."
~ *Connie Ruth Christiansen*

Thank You for:

199. _____

200. _____

201. _____

Thank You 1095
March 9

"Holding up a crisp new $100 bill, the speaker asked, "Who would like this?" Every listener eagerly raised their hand. He crumpled the bill, and asked, "Who would like *this*?" Every hand went up again. He dropped the bill onto the ground and stomped on it; grinding it into the floor with his shoe. He picked the bill up off the floor and held it in the air. Again, every hand went up. "My friends," smiled the speaker, "no matter what I did to this bill, you still wanted it because all the battering and dirt did nothing to diminish its value. You are the same. All the battering of life and the dirt on you does not diminish your worth!""
~ *Author Unknown*

"Accept and be thankful for who, what, and where you are now."
~ *Author Unknown*

Thank You for:

202. _____

203. _____

204. _____

Thank You 1095
March 10

"Delight yourself in the Lord, and He will give you the desires of your heart."
~ Psalm 37:4 NIV

"Every great dream begins with a dreamer. Always remember, you have within you the strength, the patience, and the passion to reach for the stars."
~ Harriet Tubman, African-American Slave, Union Spy, Abolitionist, Humanitarian, 1820-1913

"I am so thankful for the adventure; that God puts dreams out in front of us and then provides us the imagination, wisdom, courage and strength to chase those dreams until we catch them."
~ Connie Ruth Christiansen

Thank You for:

205. _____

206. _____

207. _____

Thank You 1095
March 11

"Give, and it shall be given unto you; good measure, pressed down, shaken together and running over."
~ Luke 6:38a NKJV

"There is a wonderful law of nature that the three things we crave most – happiness, freedom, and peace of mind are always attained by giving them to someone else."
~ Author Unknown

"Thou who hast given so much to me, give me one more thing – a grateful heart!"
~ George Herbert, English Theologian, Author, 1593-1633

Thank You for:

208. _____

209. _____

210. _____

Thank You 1095
March 12

"The inner half of every cloud is bright and shining; I therefore turn my clouds about, and always wear them inside out, to show the lining."
~ *Ellen Thorneycroft Fowler, English Teacher, Author, Poet, 1860-1929*

"At the moment of our birth, God gave each of us a song to sing. It is we who must remember that it is not how long the song, but that we sing at all. Even a grounded bird can sing, and sometimes its song is the most beautiful song of all."
~ *Vickie Girard, 1952-2007 left us too soon; and left us a legacy in her book, There's No Place Like Hope; Used by permission*

Thank You for:

211. _____

212. _____

213. _____

Thank You 1095
March 13

"I use to worry that if I was to acknowledge my blessings; if I were to say thank You, I would somehow jinx myself -- something bad would surely happen and somehow take away those blessings.

Once I recognized this disturbing belief system within myself, I saw how backwards my thinking had somehow become, and I set about to change it. I would no longer live in fear! I began to make a concerted effort to say thank You for every small and great blessing that came my way.

These days, I'm quick to express thanks whenever any good thing enters into my life. And the more I say thank You, the more good things seem to come. And now, even when blessings are not obvious, I go looking for them, just so I can give thanks."

~ Author Unknown

Thank You for:

214. _____

215. _____

216. _____

Thank You 1095
March 14

"Thanksgiving has wings and goes where it must go. Your prayer knows much more about it than you do."
~ *Victor Hugo, French Writer, Poet, Human Rights Activist, Statesman, 1802-1885*

"A single grateful thought toward heaven is the most complete prayer."
~ *Gotthold E. Lessing, German Philosopher, Publicist, Art Critic, Writer, 1729-1781*

Thank You for:

217. _____

218. _____

219. _____

Thank You 1095
March 15

"*He* is able to do immeasurably more than all we ask or imagine, according to His power that is at work within us."
~ *Ephesians 3:20 NIV*

"Trust Him when dark doubts assail you and trust Him when your strength is small. Trust Him when to simply trust seems to be the hardest thing of all. Trust Him, He is ever faithful, trust Him for His will is best."
~ *Musical Hymn written by Lucy Ann Bennett, 1850-1927*

Thank You for:

220. _____

221. _____

222. _____

Thank You 1095
March 16

"Think how different, how much more difficult our lives would be without signs.

Think on the many signs you and I have taken for granted: The isle signs in the grocery store that help us keep to our list; at our favorite fast-food drive-through to help us navigate quickly; in the bookstore to keep us from being overwhelmed by the many choices; in the mall to help us find the loo just in time; on the freeways to remind us of the speed limit and to guide us to our destination, or away from danger; on the side streets to direct the mail to our door; on the faces and in the body language of others to help us communicate well; in the sky and on the earth to remind us of our Creator.

I am thankful for signs."
~ *Connie Ruth Christiansen*

Thank You for:

223. _____

224. _____

225. _____

Thank You 1095
March 17

"We are all of us from birth to death guests at a table which we did not spread. The sun, the earth, love, friends, our very breath are parts of the banquet...Shall we think of the day as a chance to come nearer to our Host, and to find out something of Him who has fed us so long?"
~ Rebecca Harding Davis, American Author 1831-1910

"Every good and perfect gift is from above, coming down from the Father of the heavenly lights, who does not change like shifting shadows."
~ James 1:17 NIV

Thank You for:

226. _____

227. _____

228. _____

Thank You 1095
March 18

"I am grateful that no time spent with children is ever wasted."
~ *Author Unknown*

"How different would be this life without the blessing of children, without those tiny fingers and toes, the toothless smiles, the delight at every new discovery, the look of wonder on those tiny cherub faces, the giggles, the tears, the snuggles, the struggles, the accomplishments. Thank You for children."
~ *Connie Ruth Christiansen*

Thank You for:

229. _____

230. _____

231. _____

Thank You 1095
March 19

"There is a road from the eye to heart that does not go through the intellect."
~ *Gilbert K. Chesterton, British Theologian, Poet, Playwright, Journalist, 1874-1936*

"She could not see with her natural eyes, but she could see with her heart. She could not explain what a human face looked like, but she knew the face of God. Blind from six weeks old, Fanny Crosby (1820-1915) supported herself as a teacher at a blind school, and she wrote and published thousands of hymns.
Regarding her plight in life she wrote: "It seems intended by God that I should be blind, and I thank Him for the dispensation. If perfect earthly sight were offered me tomorrow I would not accept it. I might not have sung hymns to the praise of God if I had been distracted by the beautiful and interesting things about me.""
~ *Connie Ruth Christiansen*

Thank You for:

232. _____

233. _____

234. _____

Thank You 1095
March 20

"I would maintain that thanks are the highest form of thought, and that gratitude is happiness doubled by wonder."
~ *Gilbert K. Chesterton, British Theologian, Poet, Playwright, Journalist, 1874-1936*

"Time marches on; we grow older; the wonder fades as our hearts grow colder. Hold on to innocence; hold on to childhood. Remember the praise. Remember the wonder."
~ *Adapted from Big Blue Eyes, song by Connie Ruth Christiansen*

"Wonder is involuntary praise."
~ *Edward Young, English Literary Critic, Dramatist, Poet, 1683-1765*

Thank You for:

235. _____

236. _____

237. _____

Thank You 1095
March 21

"No matter how long the winter, spring is sure to follow."
~ Author Unknown

"Precious as are all the seasons of the year, none so rejoices the heart as Spring. There is about Spring a gladness that thrills the soul and lifts it up into regions of spiritual sunshine."
~ Helen Keller, American Author, Political Activist, Lecturer, blind and deaf from childhood, 1880-1968

"The breezes of spring blow gently through my body and directly into my soul."
~ Author Unknown

Thank You for:

238. _____

239. _____

240. _____

Thank You 1095
March 22

"Music takes us out of the actual and whispers to us dim secrets that startle our wonder as to who we are, and for what, whence, and whereto."
~ *Ralph Waldo Emerson, American Philosopher, Poet, 1808-1882*

"Music is the speech of angels; it is the poetry of the air. It speaks what cannot be expressed, soothes the soul and gives it rest. Music heals the heart and makes it whole; flows from heaven to the soul. Music is what feelings sound like. Thank you for music."
~ *Author Unknown*

"There's music in the sighing of a reed, there's music in the gushing of a rill;
There's music in all things, if men had ears, their earth is but an echo of the spheres."
~ *Lord Byron, Author of Don Juan, and She Walks in Beauty as the Night, 1788-1824*

Thank You for:

241. _____

242. _____

243. _____

Thank You 1095
March 23

"I am thankful for a good team. I love teamwork! Teamwork divides the task and multiplies the success."
~ *Author Unknown*

"One piece of log creates a small fire adequate to warm you up. Add just a few more pieces to blast an immense bonfire, large enough to warm up your entire circle of friends. Individuality counts but team work dynamites."
~ *Author Unknown*

"It's amazing how much you can accomplish when it doesn't matter who gets the credit."
~ *Author Unknown*

Thank You for:

244. _____

245. _____

246. _____

Thank You 1095
March 24

"The various parts that make up an airplane, each on their own, will never fly. However, assembled together, 180,000 pounds of steel and fuel can soar effortlessly through the air like a feathered bird.

Before a ship is constructed, many of its parts left alone would sink even in calm waters. But somehow collectively they stay afloat even in the worst of gales.

The pieces of us; the bitter the sweet, the sad the joyful, the heavy the light; let the Master Craftsman arrange them just so, and we are vessels that remain buoyant upon the high-water waves of life, and we have wings to rise high above life's storms."
~ *Connie Ruth Christiansen*

Thank You for:

247. _____

248. _____

249. _____

Thank You 1095
March 25

"A traveler nearing a city asked an old man seated by the road, "What are the people like in this town?" The old man replied with a question: "What were they like in the last city you visited?" "They were mean, untrustworthy, and detestable in all respects." The old man replied solemnly: "You will find them the same in the city ahead."

Another traveler stopped to make the same inquiry. Again the old man asked about the people in the place the traveler had just left. "They were fine people; honest, industrious, and generous to a fault. I was sorry to leave." The wise one responded with a smile, "So you will find them in the city ahead.""
~ Author Unknown

"Hem your blessings with thankfulness so they don't unravel."
~ Author Unknown

Thank You for:

250. _____

251. _____

252. _____

Thank You 1095
March 26

"I marvel at the courage of the shrub or little tree that struggles amongst the rocks, well knowing it can never be much more than just a scrawny scrub, yet serving in God's plot to add a little beauty to a useless barren spot. I've seen them cling tenaciously to sides of rocky bluff, as if in pure defiance of those elements so rough; or else to strive to justify audacity to choose such most unlikely habitat with odds so great to lose. They send their eager tendons out along thin veins of soil, extracting meager sustenance for their persistent toil; thus serving as a challenge to us mortals who complain about the petty hardships that we often entertain."
   ~ Carl D. Rollins, Author of Yesterday Today and Tomorrow, 1888-1966

"A hero is no braver than an ordinary man, but he is brave five minutes longer."
   ~ Ralph Waldo Emerson, American Philosopher, Poet, 1808-1882

Thank You for:

253. _____

254. _____

255. _____

Thank You 1095
March 27

"One evening as I was picking the toys up off the floor I noticed a small hand print on the wall beside the door. I knew that it was something I had seen most every day, but this time when I saw it there, I wanted it to stay; and tears welled up inside my eyes. I knew it wouldn't last, for every mother knows her children grow up way too fast. I put my chores aside and held my children tight; I sang to them sweet lullabies and rocked them through the night. Sometimes we take for granted all those things that seem so small, like one of God's great treasures... a small hand print on the wall."
~ *Author Unknown*

"Be thankful for and enjoy the seemingly insignificant things of life, for one day you may look back and realize they are the treasures."
~ *Author Unknown*

Thank You for:

256. _____

257. _____

258. _____

Thank You 1095
March 28

Every natural fact is a symbol of some spiritual fact."
~ *Ralph Waldo Emerson, American Philosopher, Poet, 1808-1882*

"For the joy of ear and eye, for the heart and mind's delight, for the mystic harmony, linking sense to sound and sight; Lord of all, to Thee we raise, this our hymn of grateful praise."
~ *From For the Beauty of the Earth, hymn by Folliott Piermont, Teacher, Writer, Poet, 1835-1917*

Thank You for:

259. _____

260. _____

261. _____

Thank You 1095
March 29

"A cheerful heart is a good medicine."
~ *Proverbs 17:22 NIV*

"How true it is that, if we are cheerful and contented, all nature smiles, the air seems more balmy, the sky clearer, the earth has a brighter green, the flowers are more fragrant, and the sun, moon, and stars all appear more beautiful, and seem to rejoice with us."
~ *Orison Swett Marden, M.D., Author, Philosopher, Theologian, 1850-1924*

"A friendly look, a kindly smile, one thankful act, and life's worthwhile."
~ *Author Unknown*

Thank You for:

262. _____

263. _____

264. _____

Thank You 1095
March 30

"Heard melodies are sweet. Those unheard are sweeter."
~ *John Keates, English Romantic Poet, 1795-1821*

"Croaking frog, creaking cricket, buzzing bee; chirping bird, whistling wind, rustling leaves; purring cat, crackling fire, bubbling brook, dropping rain. Ears to hear, many sounds, joy to me!"
~ *From Joy to Me; a children's song and book by Connie Ruth Christiansen*

"Everyone hears only what he understands."
~ *Johann Wolfgang von Goethe, German Writer and Polymath, 1749-1832*

Thank You for:

265. _____

266. _____

267. _____

Thank You 1095
March 31

"When you feel like giving up, remember and be thankful for the reason you held on so long in the first place – and remember that although you are not there yet, you are closer than you were yesterday."
~ *Author Unknown*

"Talent, genius and education will not take the place of persistence and determination. Be thankful that anyone can succeed with persistence and determination."
~ *Lisah Quinn VandeRiet and husband John are Missionaries to Russia and other countries; Used by permission*

"Every accomplishment starts with the decision to try. And if at first you don't succeed, be thankful that you can try, try again."
~ *Author Unknown*

Thank You for:

268. _____

269. _____

270. _____

Thank You 1095
April 1

"What is lovely never dies, but passes into other loveliness."
~ *Thomas Bailey Aldrich, American Writer, Poet, Editor, 1836-1907*

"Let me not fear the darkness now, since Life and Light break through *Your* tomb; Teach me that doubts no more oppress, no more consume. Show me that *You* are April Lord, and *You* the flowers and the grass; Then when awake the soft spring winds, I will hear *You* pass."
~ *Charles Hanson Towne, American Editor, Author, Poet, 1877-1949*

"Oh death where is your sting? Oh grave, where is your victory?"
~ *I Corinthians 15:55 NKJB*

Thank You for:

271. _____

272. _____

273. _____

Thank You 1095
April 2

"Life is a never ending cycle of love exchanges that fit together in a synchronized puzzle – each opportunity to love grants lessons and mistakes to learn from, people and situations to be thankful for.

I am thankful for those who granted me mistakes; unconditionally caring for me through trial and tribulation; every storm and dark day. If it had not been for them I would not have known how to love, nor how to accept love."
~ Macque Linder, Poet, Winner of the 2009 ACT-SO National Poetry Contest; Used by permission

"Love is to the heart what the summer is to the farmer's year - it brings to harvest all the loveliest flowers of the soul."
~Author Unknown

Thank You for:

274. _____

275. _____

276. _____

Thank You 1095
April 3

"They who sow in tears shall reap with songs of joy."
~ Psalm 126:5 NIV

"I have held many things in my hands, and I have lost them all; but whatever I have placed in God's hands; that I still possess."
~ Martin Luther, German Theologian who initiated the Protestant Reformation, 1483-1546

"Judge each day not by the harvest you reap but by the seeds you plant."
~ Robert Louis Stevenson, Scottish Author of Dr. Jekyll & Mr. Hyde, and Treasure Island, 1850-1894

Thank You for:

277. _____

278. _____

279. _____

Thank You 1095
April 4

"Be still and know that I am God."
~ *Psalm 46:10a KJV*

"In the rush and noise of life, as you have intervals, step home within yourselves and be still; wait upon God, and feel His good presence; this will carry you evenly through your day's business."
~ *William Penn, Philosopher, Founder of the Province of Pennsylvania, 1644-1718*

"Quiet minds cannot be perplexed or frightened, but go on in fortune or misfortune at their own private pace, like a clock during a thunderstorm."
~ *Robert Louis Stevenson, Author of Dr. Jekyll and Mr. Hyde, and Treasure Island, 1850-1894*

Thank You for:

280. _____

281. _____

282. _____

Thank You 1095
April 5

"This is the day the Lord has made. We will rejoice and be glad in it."
~ *Psalm 118:24 NLT*

"Receive every day as a resurrection from death, as a new enjoyment of life; meet every rising sun with such sentiments of God's goodness, as if you hadn't seen it, and all things, new-created upon your account: and under the sense of so great a blessing, let your joyful heart praise and magnify so good and glorious a Creator."
~ *William Law, English Theologian, Mystic, Writer, 1687-1761*

Thank You for:

283. _____

284. _____

285. _____

Thank You 1095
April 6

"God is good, God is great, and we thank Him for this food. By His hand must all be fed; Give us Lord our daily bread."
~ *Traditional mealtime prayer, Author Unknown*

"I say grace before meals, and say grace before the concert and the opera, and grace before the play and pantomime, and grace before I open a book, and grace before sketching, painting, swimming, fencing, boxing, walking, playing, dancing, and grace before I dip the pen in the ink."
~ *Gilbert K. Chesterton, British Theologian, Poet, Playwright, Journalist, 1874-1936*

"Rejoice always. Pray without ceasing."
~ *I Thessalonians 5:15-18 NASB*

Thank You for:

286. _____

287. _____

288. _____

Thank You 1095
April 7

"The little cares that fretted me, I lost them yesterday among the fields above the sea, among the winds at play, among the lowing of the herds, the rustling of the trees, among the singing of the birds, the humming of the bees.

The foolish fears of what may pass I cast them all away, among the clover-scented grass, among the new mown hay, among the hushing of the corn where drowsy poppies nod, where ill thoughts die and good are born, out in the fields with God."
~ Elizabeth Barrett Browning, Victorian English Poet; wife of Robert Browning, 1806-1861

"The best remedy for those who are afraid, lonely or unhappy is to go outside, somewhere where they can be quiet, alone with the heavens, nature and God. Because only then does one feel that all is as it should be."
~ Annelies Marie (Anne) Frank, Jewish child victim of the Nazi WWII Holocaust, 1929-1945

Thank You for:

289. _____

290. _____

291. _____

Thank You 1095
April 8

"God - the greatest lover
So loved – the greatest degree
The world – the greatest company
That He gave – the greatest act
His only begotten Son – the greatest gift
That whosoever – the greatest opportunity
Believeth – the greatest simplicity
In Him – the greatest attraction
Should not perish – the greatest promise
But – the greatest difference
Have – the greatest certainty
Eternal life – the greatest possession."
~ Adapted from John 3:16 by Davies, British Engineer, Politician, Author, 1767-1839

"The world will never starve for want of wonders."
~ Gilbert K. Chesterton, British Theologian, Poet, Playwright, Journalist, 1874-1936

Thank You for:

292. _____

293. _____

294. _____

Thank You 1095
April 9

"A discouraged little boy was telling of his many troubles. While she was listening, Grandma was frosting a chocolate cake. When the boy came to the end of his list of woes, Grandma asked if he would like a snack, to which of course he agreed. "Want some cooking oil?" she asked. "Yuck!" said the boy. "Well then, how about a couple of raw eggs?" He wrinkled up his face, "Gross, Grandma!" She smiled and asked, "Some flour? Or maybe baking soda?" The boy frowned, "Grandma, those are all icky!"

She turned and answered, "By themselves, yes. But if you mix them together, they make a delicious cake! When we have many troubles, we wonder why God would allow such trouble. But then He mixes the troubles together and makes something great!" The little boy pondered her words of wisdom as he happily devoured his cake."
~ Author Unknown

Thank You for:

295. _____

296. _____

297. _____

Thank You 1095
April 10

"My grace is sufficient for you, for My power is made perfect in weakness."
~ *2 Corinthians 12:9 NKJV*

"Remember that your work comes only moment by moment, and as surely as God calls you to work, He gives the strength to do it."
~ *Priscilla Maurice, Victorian era Author of Sickness, Its Trials and Blessings, 1775-1854*

"All God's giants have been weak men who did great things for God because they reckoned on God being with them."
~ *J. Hudson Taylor, British Missionary, Founder of the Inland China Mission, 1832-1905*

Thank You for:

298. _____

299. _____

300. _____

Thank You 1095
April 11

"Whenever I wonder *what if?* I mostly don't find an answer. So I turn that wondering around and change it into a thank You.

For Instance: What if there were no reflections, what if there were no mirrors?

Thank You for reflections, thank You for reflectors; for the shine of the moon because of the sun; for mountains piled up one on top of the other, some towering to the sky, some reflected in the crystal clear river water below; for a mirror to see myself in the morning, maybe not liking so much what I see, but having a reference to adjust it; for seeing myself in the face of another when they look at me with admiration or love; for seeing myself in the face of another when maybe I don't like what I see, but having a reference to adjust it; for the gift of being a mirror myself; for the potential to be a reflection of God."
~ *Connie Ruth Christiansen*

Thank You for:

301. _____

302. _____

303. _____

Thank You 1095
April 12

"By wisdom a house is built, and through understanding it is established; through knowledge its rooms are filled with rare and beautiful treasures."
~ *Proverbs 24:3-4 NIV*

"No great thing is built suddenly, any more than a bunch of grapes or a fig. If you tell me that you desire a fig, I answer you that there must be time. Let it first blossom, then bear fruit, then ripen."
~ *Epictetus, Greek Philosopher, Teacher, 55-135 AD*

"Time is the wisest counselor of all."
~ *Pericles, Greek Statesman, General, Orator 495-429 BC*

Thank You for:

304. _____

305. _____

306. _____

Thank You 1095
April 13

"When we share laughter, there's twice the fun; when we share success, we surpass what we've done.

When we share problems, there's half the pain; when we share tears, a rainbow follows rain.

When we share dreams, they become real; when we share secrets, it's our hearts we reveal.

If we share a smile, then our love shows; if we share a hug, then our love grows.

If we share with someone on whom we depend, that person becomes family or friend.

And what draws us closer and makes us all care, isn't what we have, but the things that we share."

~ *Author Unknown*

Thank You for:

307. _____

308. _____

309. _____

You 1095
April 14

"In a very real sense, each one of us, as humans beings, have been given a golden cup filled with potential and dreams, and with love, warmth, and kisses, hugs, blessings from our children, family members, friends, pets, even strangers, and above all it is filled with an unconditional love from God. There is simply no other possession, anyone could hold, more precious than this cup."
~ *Author Unknown*

"The optimist says the cup is half full. The pessimist says the cup is half empty. The child of thanksgiving says, my cup runs over."
~ *Author Unknown*

Thank You for:

310. _____

311. _____

312. _____

Thank You 1095
April 15

"Happiness is as a butterfly, which when pursued, is always beyond our grasp, but which if you will sit down quietly, may alight upon you."
~ Nathaniel Hawthorne, American Novelist and Short Story Writer, 1804-1864

"Life isn't about waiting for the storm to pass, it's about learning to dance in the rain."
~ Author Unknown

"O Thou, whose bounty fills my cup with every blessing meet. I give Thee thanks for every drop, the bitter and the sweet."
~ Jane Crewdson, Poet, Daughter of George Fox, 1808-1863

Thank You for:

313. _____

314. _____

315. _____

Thank You 1095
April 16

"When was the last time you lounged on a hillside to watch white fluffy clouds move lazily across the blue, or peaked out from under an umbrella to see them gray-black and racing towards each other in a thunderstorm? How long since you stood in the dark of night and gazed into the vastness, taking in the wonder of the moon, the stars? When did you last look up? And when did you last look down to note the finery at your feet? How truly amazing the earth we walk upon; how incredible our heavenly covering."
~ *Connie Ruth Christiansen*

"God writes the Gospel not in the Bible alone, but on trees, flowers, clouds, and stars."
~ *Martin Luther, German Theologian who initiated the Protestant Reformation, 1483-1546*

Thank You for:

316. _____

317. _____

318. _____

Thank You 1095
April 17

"Science will never be able to reduce the value of a sunset to arithmetic. Nor can it reduce friendship to formula. Laughter and love, pain and loneliness, the challenge of beauty and truth; these will always surpass the scientific mastery of nature."
~ *Dr. Louis Orr, 1899-1976; excerpt from his 1960 American Medical Association convention speech*

"I once had a sparrow alight upon my shoulder, while hoeing in a village garden, and I felt I was more distinguished by that circumstance than I should have been by any epaulet I could have worn."
~ *Henry David Thoreau, Author, Poet, Naturalist, Abolitionist, Philosopher, 1817-1862*

Thank You for:

319. _____

320. _____

321. _____

Thank You 1095
April 18

"Forgive us our debts as we forgive our debtors."
~ Matthew 6:12 KJV

"Forgiveness is the answer to the child's dream of a miracle by which what is broken is made whole again, what is soiled is made clean again."
~ Dag Hammarskjold, Swedish Diplomat, Economist, Author, the only posthumous Nobel Prize winner, 1905-1961

"How thankful I am that to forgive is to set a prisoner free and then to discover that the prisoner was me."
~ Author Unknown

Thank You for:

322. _____

323. _____

324. _____

Thank You 1095
April 19

"The soul would have no rainbow had the eyes no tears."
~ *John Vance Cheney, American Poet, Essayist, Librarian, 1828-1922*

"Heaven knows we need never be ashamed of our tears, for they are rain upon the blinding dust of earth, overlying our hard hearts."
~ *Charles Dickens, Author of Oliver Twist, A Christmas Carol, and Great Expectations, 1812-1870*

"There is a sacredness in tears. They are not the mark of weakness, but of power. They speak more eloquently than ten thousand tongues."
~ *Washington Irving, American Historian, Author of Sleepy Hollow, and Rip Van Winkle, 1783-1859*

Thank You for:
325. _____

326. _____

327. _____

Thank You 1095
April 20

"Your thank you may be the only gratitude someone will hear. Your kindness may be the only encouragement someone will receive. Your life may be the only Bible someone reads."
~Author Unknown

"I would be true, for there are those who trust me; I would be pure, for there are those who care. I would be strong, for there is much to suffer; I would be brave, for there is much to dare. I would be friend of all, to foe, the friendless; I would be humble for I know my weakness. I would look up, and laugh, and love, and lift."
~ From a Hymn by Howard Arnold Walter, Pastor, Teacher, Missionary, 1883-1918

Thank You for:

328. _____

329. _____

330. _____

Thank You 1095
April 21

"Each one of us is building upon the legacy of another. Remember and be thankful for those who have given us the example of a thankful heart; who have taught us that faith can turn potential into power; who have passed through this life freely sharing the fruit of their dreams.

Each of us eventually will leave behind a legacy as we pass from this earth. We are busy building that legacy now. Be thankful that as long as we have breath we can add to that legacy; we can ask these questions, and make the best choices: *Will I leave behind thanksgiving or bitterness? Will I be remembered for my great untapped potential or for stepping out in faith and reaching a portion of that potential? Will I pass from this life holding tight to my dreams or will I let go to leave bits and pieces of them behind for others to enjoy and to build upon?*

Be thankful that it is not too late to leave a gift of something good following behind."
~ Connie Ruth Christiansen

Thank You for:

331. _____

332. _____

333. _____

Thank You 1095
April 22

"There will always be another day to say I love you. But just in case I might be wrong, and today is all I get, I'd like to say how much I love you and may we never forget that tomorrow is not promised to anyone, young or old alike, and today may be the last chance you get to hold your loved ones tight. So if you're waiting for tomorrow, why not do it today? For if tomorrow never comes, you will surely regret the day that you didn't take that extra time for a smile, a hug, or a kiss, and that you were too busy to grant someone, what turned out to be their one last wish.

So hold your loved ones close today, whisper in their ear; Tell them how much you love them and that you'll always hold them dear; Take time to say "I'm sorry, please forgive me, thank you, or it's okay." Then if tomorrow never comes, you'll have no regrets about today."
~ Author Unknown

Thank You for:

334. _____

335. _____

336. _____

Thank You 1095
April 23

"Be happy with those who are happy, and weep with those who weep."
~ *Romans 12:15 NLT*

"To be able to find joy in another's joy, that is the secret of happiness."
~ *George Bernanos, Award winning French Author, 1888-1948*

"And let us be grateful to people who make us happy, they are the charming gardeners who make our souls blossom."
~ *Marcel Proust, French Novelist, Critic, Essayist, 1871-1922*

Thank You for:

337. _____

338. _____

339. _____

Thank You 1095
April 24

"The heavens declare the glory of God; the skies proclaim the work of His hands."
Psalm 19:1 NIV

"Something for you to ponder, and while pondering, let the wonder and thanksgiving flow:
There is a very tiny light in the night sky, barely visible to the human eye, situated close to the left-hand corner of the star formation called Pegasus. That little spot of light represents the immense Spiral Galaxy of Andromeda. Andromeda is as large as our Galaxy the Milky Way; it is 750,000 light-years away; it is one of a hundred million known galaxies; and it consists of one hundred billion suns, each one larger than the sun that our earth orbits.
The same Creator of this tiny light in the sky, this star amongst billions of stars, is the Creator of our life here on earth."
~ Author Unknown

Thank You for:

340. _____

341. _____

342. _____

Thank You 1095
April 25

"A man should learn to detect and watch that gleam of light which flashes across his mind from within."
~ *Ralph Waldo Emerson, American Philosopher, Poet, 1808-1882*

"Thomas Edison recorded 10,000 aborted attempts before he successfully invented the light bulb. Be thankful Mr. Edison had the light from candles in order to work well into the night.

Be thankful for the light bulb. Be thankful for the light of imagination. Be thankful that we can be lights in a dark world. Be thankful for light."
~ *Connie Ruth Christiansen*

Thank You for:

343. _____

344. _____

345. _____

Thank You 1095
April 26

"If we allow some area of our life to spin out of control, God will continue to bring it up until we deal with it. Ultimately, God will allow nothing to escape; every detail of our lives is under His scrutiny. God will bring us back in countless ways to the same point over and over again. And He never tires of bringing us back to that one point until we learn the lesson, because His purpose is to produce the finished product. Beware of becoming careless over the small details of life and saying, "Oh, that will have to do for now." Whatever it may be, God will point it out with persistence until we become entirely His."
~ Oswald Chambers, Scottish Minister, Teacher, Author of My Utmost for His Highest, 1874-1917

"Good, better, best, never let it rest till your good is better and your better is best."
~ Author Unknown

Thank You for:

346. _____

347. _____

348. _____

Thank You 1095
April 27

"Do not waste time not being thankful. Do not waste time not being happy. Do not waste time thinking about quitting. If one window closes, run to another window, or use your God given strength to break down a door."
~ *Author Unknown*

"Nothing can stop the man with the right mental attitude from achieving his goal. Nothing on earth can help the man with the wrong mental attitude."
~ *Thomas Jefferson, 3rd President of the United States, 1743-1826*

Thank You for:

349. _____

350. _____

351. _____

Thank You 1095
April 28

"For going up and for coming down, for mountains, hills and valleys, for staircase steps and ladders, escalators, elevators;

For climbing upward, coasting downward, sliding, diving, jumping, for somewhere fun to go up to, and somewhere safe to go down to;

For seeds that are under and then they grow upward, for growing up and older from first being smaller and younger;

For lifted up hope when spirits are down, for lifted up head, a smile from a frown;

For the above of the heavens and the down of the earth, for being here now and up there ever after; Thank You for up, thank You for down."
~ Connie Ruth Christiansen

Thank You for:

352. _____

353. _____

354. _____

Thank You 1095
April 29

"More sky than man can see, more seas than he can sail, more sun than he can bear to watch, more stars than he can scale. More breath than he can breathe, more yield than he can sow, more grace than he can comprehend, more love than he can know – The extravagance of God."
~ *Dr. Ralph W. Seager, College Professor, Author and Poet, 1911-2008*

"I still find each day too short for all the thoughts I want to think, all the walks I want to take, all the books I want to read, and all the friends I want to see. The longer I live the more my mind dwells upon the beauty and the wonder of the world."
~ *John Burroughs, American Naturalist, Philosopher, Writer, 1837-1921*

Thank You for:

355. _____

356. _____

357. _____

Thank You 1095
April 30

"Last night my little boy confessed to me, some childish wrong, and kneeling at my knee, he prayed with tears, "Dear God, make me a man like Daddy, wise and strong...I know I can."

Then while he slept, I knelt beside his bed, confessed my sins and prayed with humbled low-bowed head, "Oh God, make me a child, like my child here; pure guileless, trusting You with faith sincere...I know I can.""
~ Andrew Gillies, 1870-1942

"We try to teach our children all about life, but it is actually they who are teaching us what life is all about."
~ Author Unknown

Thank You for:

358. _____

359. _____

360. _____

Thank You 1095
May 1

"My job upon awaking is to choose the profile of my day -- I decide.

I can complain because the weather is rainy or be thankful that the grass is getting watered for free; I can whine because I have to go to work or I can appreciate that I have a job to do; I can grumble about my health or I can rejoice that I am alive; I can mourn lack or loss of friends or I can embark upon a quest of new relationships; I can protest that I have housework or be grateful that God has provided shelter.

Today stretches before me, waiting to be shaped. I am the sculptor, I get to choose."
~ Author Unknown

"Most of the shadows of this life are caused by our standing in our own sunshine."
~ Ralph Waldo Emerson, American Philosopher, Poet, 1808-1882

Thank You for:

361. _____

362. _____

363. _____

Thank You 1095
May 2

"Great things are done by a series of small things brought together."
~ *Vincent van Gogh, Dutch post-impressionist Painter, 1853-1890*

"Success in life is founded upon attention towards the small things rather than the large things; to the every-day things nearest to us rather than to the things that are remote and uncommon."
~ *Booker T. Washington, African American Slave, Educator, Author, Orator, Political Leader, 1856-1915*

"Be faithful in small things because it is in them that your strength lies."
~ *Mother Teresa, Catholic Nun, founder of the Missionaries of Charity in Kolkata, India, 1910-1997*

Thank You for:

364. _____

365. _____

366. _____

Thank You 1095
May 3

"Be thankful that you don't have everything you desire, so that you have something to look forward to. Be thankful you don't know everything or you wouldn't have the opportunity to learn and to grow. Be thankful for your limitations, because they give you opportunities for improvement. Be thankful for each new challenge that will build your strength, character, and patience. Be thankful for your mistakes and for the valuable lessons your disappointments teach you. Be thankful for your troubles and they will become your blessings."
~ *Author Unknown*

"If you haven't all the things you want, be thankful for the things you don't have that you wouldn't want."
~ *Author Unknown*

Thank You for:

367. _____

368. _____

369. _____

Thank You 1095
May 4

"Men come and go; leaders, teachers, and thinkers speak and work for a season, and then fall silent and impotent. He abides. They die, but He lives. They are lights kindled, and therefore, sooner or later quenched; but He is the true light from which they draw all their brightness, and He shines for evermore."
~ *Alexander MacLaren, English Preacher, Expositor, 1826 -1910*

"Praise be to the name of God for ever and ever; wisdom and power are His. He changes times and seasons; He deposes kings and raises up others. He gives wisdom to the wise and knowledge to the discerning. He reveals deep and hidden things; He knows what lies in darkness, and light dwells in Him."
~ *Daniel 2:20-22 NIV*

Thank You for:

370. _____

371. _____

372. _____

Thank You 1095
May 5

"Yesterday a butterfly floated through the sky, soared through the atmosphere, then drifted close enough to hear. I said, "I would love to fly with you and sail around the way you do. It looks like it would be such fun to fly toward the summer sun. But I haven't wings, just these two arms; my human feet must touch ground."

Then magically he spoke to me and told me what his wish would be. "What I would love most to do is walk upon God's Earth with you; to squish its mud between my toes, or touch my finger to my nose. But I don't have legs that swing; I haven't arms, just these two wings."

And so we went our separate ways in wonder and surprise; for we had seen Gods precious gifts through someone else's eyes."
~ *Author Unknown*

Thank You for:

373. _____

374. _____

375. _____

Thank You 1095
May 6

"Always remember to forget the things that made you sad but never forget to remember the things that made you glad.

Always remember to forget the friends that proved untrue but don't forget to remember those who have stuck by you.

Always to remember to forget the troubles that have passed away but never forget to remember the blessings that come each day."
~ Author Unknown

"Every year of my life I grow more convinced that it is wisest and best to fix our attention on the beautiful and the good, and dwell as little as possible on the evil and the false."
~ Richard Cecil, American Clergyman, 1748-1810

Thank You for:

376. _____

377. _____

378. _____

Thank You 1095
May 7

"The best gift you can give is a hug. One size fits all and no one minds if you return it."
~ *Author Unknown*

"Happy hugs, Powder hugs, Big round squishy squashy hugs; Guy hugs, Girl hugs, Twitchy twatchy spaztic hugs; Flower hugs, Scented hugs, Tall skinny beanpole hugs; Crunchy hugs, Veggie hugs, I will never let you go hugs; Puppy hugs, Kitty hugs, Falling in the snow hugs; Hugs, hugs, happy hugs, I really, really like hugs. Thank You for hugs."
~ *Author Unknown*

"A hug delights and warms and charms; that must be why God gave us arms."
~ *Author Unknown*

Thank You for:

379. _____

380. _____

381. _____

Thank You 1095
May 8

"Clothing fashion may interest you, or not. But if you think about it at all you will find apparel to be thankful for, and that just might make you smile.

Belts and suspenders and ties for looks or to hold something together or up; boots that match or to keep off the rain and the mud; scarves and mittens for color or to keep you warm; uniforms that let you know who the nurse or the waitress is, or that the man with his head under your car hood belongs there; zippers and buttons and seams placed just so to make you look slimmer and sweeter, or bigger and bolder; lengths and shapes that allow you to reveal on the outside just a glimpse of who you are on the inside; and then there are the things that shine and sparkle; I am thankful for things that sparkle, and for fashion variety, practical and otherwise."
~ *Connie Ruth Christiansen*

Thank You for:

382. _____

383. _____

384. _____

Thank You 1095
May 9

"Just up the road from my home is a field, with two horses in it. From a distance, each horse looks like any other horse, but if you get closer you will notice that one of the horses is blind. And if you keep watching and listening you will see that the other horse has a bell tied around his neck so that the blind horse will be able to hear where his friend is going; so he can follow. If you take precious time to remain watching, you will see that the small horse with the bell is continually looking back to make sure his large blind friend isn't too far behind to hear the bell; especially when they are making their way safely to the barn for food and shelter.

Like the owner of these two horses, God does not throw us away because we are blind or imperfect. He watches over us and brings others into our lives to help us with our needs; to help us find the way. Sometimes we are the blind horse; sometimes He lets us be the horse with the bell."
~ Author Unknown

Thank You for:

385. _____

386. _____

387. _____

Thank You 1095
May 10

"A story is told of a king who had a boulder placed as a blockade upon a roadway. Then he hid himself to watch and see if anyone would remove the huge rock. Some people climbed around it, some complained about it, but did nothing to remove it. Some of the complainers were wealthy and strong with good resources to move it.

Then along came a poor old man carrying a load of vegetables. He laid down his burden and pushed and strained until he moved the obstruction from the road. He turned and noticed a package lying in the road where the bolder had been. The package contained many gold coins and a note from the king indicating that the gold was for the person who took the effort to remove the blockade.

This peasant learned what many others never seem to understand: Every obstacle presents an opportunity to improve ones' present condition."
~ Author Unknown

Thank You for:

388. _____

389. _____

390. _____

Thank You 1095
May 11

"What if God decided to stop blessing me today because I forgot to thank Him yesterday? What if I never saw another flower bloom because I grumbled when He sent rain? What if He took His written Word away tomorrow because I didn't read it today? What if He would not listen to me because I refuse to listen to Him? What if He stopped loving me because I stopped loving another of His creation? What if He answered my prayers the way I obey His directives? I am thankful God's blessings are based on His goodness, and not based on what I do or do not do."
~ *Author Unknown*

"He blesses us because He is good, not because of any evil we have avoided, or for any good we have done."
~ *Author Unknown*

Thank You for:

391. _____

392. _____

393. _____

Thank You 1095
May 12

"I am thankful for my mother, every single day; I'm thankful for her support every step of the way; I'm thankful for the patience that she always shows; I'm thankful for my mother, more than anybody knows.

I'm thankful for my home, the love and peace that dwell there; I'm thankful for my siblings whom I will always hold dear; I'm thankful for my knowledge and everything I have, like the chance to go to college and follow my own path.

I'm thankful for my teacher and all that she has done, such as always being positive and making our class fun. So now I will say like I've said many times before: I know I am truly blessed, and have a lot to be thankful for."

~ Taylor Christine Whitmore, 17 years old, 3/2011; Used by permission

Thank You for:

394. _____

395. _____

396. _____

Thank You 1095
May 13

"I walk down the path, heavy of heart, until I notice the flowers, looking up; calling out: "Here we are! We were once but seeds in the dark, and now look, we are color, and light, and joy.""
~ *Connie Ruth Christiansen*

"We may pass violets looking for roses. We may pass contentment looking for victory."
~ *Author Unknown*

"God will work all things together for good for those who love Him and are called according to His purpose."
~ *Romans 8:28 NKJV*

Thank You for:

397. _____

398. _____

399. _____

Thank You 1095
May 14

"The poetry of the earth is never dead."
~ *John Keates, English Romantic Poet, 1795-1821*

"See the world in a grain of sand and Heaven in a wildflower, hold infinity in the palm of your hand and eternity in an hour."
~ *William Blake, English Romantic Poet and Painter, 1757-1827*

"I love to think of nature as an unlimited broadcasting station, through which God speaks to us every hour, if we will only tune in."
~ *George Washington Carver, African-American Slave, Scientist, Botanist, Educator, Inventor, 1864-1943*

Thank You for:

400. _____

401. _____

402. _____

Thank You 1095
May 15

"We often choose joys and sorrows long before we experience them."
~ *Khalil Gibran, Lebanese American Artist, Poet, Author of The Prophet, 1883-1931*

"When one door closes another opens; but we often look so long and regretfully at the closed door that we don't see the door opened to us."
~ *Alexander Graham Bell, Scientist, Inventor, 1847-1922*

"I have set before you life and death, the blessing and the curse. So choose life."
~ *Deuteronomy 30:19 NASB*

Thank You for:

403. _____

404. _____

405. _____

Thank You 1095
May 16

"As iron sharpens iron, so one man sharpens another."
~ Proverbs 27:17 NIV

"I am thankful for people who help to keep me balanced. To have a close honest group of friends such as those of a work or church family helps me to keep a sky in my life and to look up; to keep my hand in God's and to hold on to Him; to see the eternal values above the material; to lift life above myself to service; to see the good in others and to praise it; to keep sweet and to keep busy for Him; to have a seeing eye, a feeling heart and a helping hand; to test the motive of life and to choose the best; to do justly, love mercy, be thankful, and to walk humbly."
~ Author Unknown

Thank You for:
406. _____

407. _____

408. _____

Thank You 1095
May 17

"Life may be too short to live out all of your many dreams, but life is not too short to love the people who pass your way. And life is not too short to be thankful."
~ Author Unknown

"Don't defer living to an arbitrary point in the future. Don't save any dream for a special occasion. Being alive is the special occasion.

Be thankful for now -- make it so beautiful it will be worth remembering. Life is not measured by the number of breaths we take, but by the moments that take our breath away."
~ Author Unknown

"Forever is composed of nows."
~ Emily Dickinson, American Poet, 1830-1886

Thank You for:

409. _____

410. _____

411. _____

Thank You 1095
May 18

"Let us be like a bird for a moment perched on a frail branch while he sings. Though he feels it bend, yet he sings his song, knowing that he has wings."
~ *Victor Hugo, French Statesman, Poet, Playwright, Artist, Human Rights Activist, 1802-1885*

"If ever you have a big problem, don't say: "God, I have a big problem." Instead say: "Problem, I have a big God!""
~ *Author Unknown*

"He who sacrifices thank offerings honors Me, and he prepares the way so that I may show him the salvation of God."
~ *Psalm 50:23 NIV*

Thank You for:

412. _____

413. _____

414. _____

Thank You 1095
May 19

"Gratitude is the sign of noble souls."
~ Aesop, a Greek slave accredited with a collection of stories known as Aesop's Fables, 620-540 BC

"To approach my work with a clean mind; to hold ever before me, even in the doing of little things, the Ultimate Purpose toward which I am working; to meet men and women with laughter on my lips and love in my heart; to be gentle kind, thankful and courteous through all the hours; to approach the night with weariness that ever woos sleep, and the joy that comes from work well done. This is how I desire to waste wisely my days."
~ Thomas Dekker, English Elizabethan Playwright and Pamphleteer, 1570-1632

Thank You for:

415. _____

416. _____

417. _____

Thank You 1095
May 20

Be thankful that even a pencil can teach us valuable life lessons:

"The Pencil Maker took the pencil aside, and just before putting him into the box he said: "There are 5 things you need to know in order to become the best pencil you can be.

One: You will be able to do many great things, but only if you allow yourself to be held in someone's hands.

Two: You will experience a painful sharpening from time to time, but you'll need it to become a better pencil.

Three: You have the tools to correct any mistake you might make.

Four: The most important part of you will always be what's inside.

Five: On every writing surface, you must leave your mark – No matter what obstacles, you must continue to write.""

~ Author Unknown

Thank You for:

418. _____

419. _____

420. _____

Thank You 1095
May 21

"I may never see tomorrow; there's no written guarantee. And things that happened yesterday belong to history. I cannot predict the future, I cannot change the past. I have just this present moment; I must treat it as my last.

The unkind things I do today may never be undone; and friendships that I fail to win may nevermore be won. I may not have another chance on bended knee to pray and thank God with humble heart for giving me this day."
~ *Author Unknown*

"The past cannot be altered. Even God Himself will not change the truth of the past. The good news is this: while you may not have the ability to change the truth of your past, you do have the ability to change the truth of your future."
~ *Connie Ruth Christiansen*

Thank You for:

421. _____

422. _____

423. _____

Thank You 1095
May 22

"For every knee that bowed to dig in the dirt, planting bulbs in the autumn and seeds in the spring, and remembered to water at just the right time, and to remove the weeds that might hinder my view as I pass by and drink in the miracle; for neighbors and gardeners who took the time, thank you."
~ *Connie Christiansen*

"Sometimes our light goes out but is blown into flame by another human being. Each of us owes deepest thanks to those who have rekindled this light."
~ *Albert Schweitzer, Franco-German Theologian, Organist, Philosopher, Physician, 1875-1965*

Thank You for:

424. _____

425. _____

426. _____

Thank You 1095
May 23

"Never lose an opportunity to see anything that is beautiful. It is God's handwriting; a wayside sacrament. Welcome it in every fair face, every fair sky, every fair flower."
~ *Ralph Waldo Emerson, American Philosopher, Poet, 1808-1882*

"What a joy it is to feel the soft, springy earth under my feet once more, to follow grassy roads that lead to ferny brooks where I can bathe my fingers in a cataract of rippling notes, or to clamber over a stone wall into green fields that tumble and roll and climb in riotous gladness!"
~ *Helen Keller, American Author, Political Activist, Lecturer, blind and deaf from childhood, 1880-1968*

Thank You for:

427. _____

428. _____

429. _____

Thank You 1095
May 24

"A grateful heart is one that finds the countless blessings of God in the seeming ordinary of everyday life."
~ *Author Unknown*

"Read a book, take a trip to the museum, drive along a country road, hike into the hills, take a walk in the park, breathe deeply the fresh air, feel the grass beneath your feet, dip your bare feet into a puddle, dig your toes into the mud, listen to the sounds of water, listen to the sounds of birds, listen to music, look at old photos, watch your pet sleeping in the sun, watch a child at play, get up, get out, open up your eyes; take note of the multiple resources, beauty, and trivia of your home, your community, of this earth, and be prompted to thanksgiving."
~ *Connie Ruth Christiansen*

Thank You for:

430. _____

431. _____

432. _____

Thank You 1095
May 25

"Live well, learn plenty, laugh often, love much."
~ *Ralph Waldo Emerson, American Philosopher, Poet, 1808-1882*

"When I dance, I dance, when I sleep, I sleep; yes, and when I walk alone in a beautiful orchard, if my thoughts drift to far-off matters for some part of the time, for some other part I lead them back again to the walk, the orchard, to the sweetness of this solitude, to myself."
~ *Michel Eyquem de Montaigne, French Renaissance Writer, 1533-1592*

"If you have much, give of your wealth; if you have little, give of your heart. Give always of your thanks."
~ *Ancient Arabian Proverb*

Thank You for:

433. _____

434. _____

435. _____

Thank You 1095
May 26

"Faith comes by hearing, and hearing by the word of God."
~ *Romans 10:17 NKJV*

"It is not at all incredible, that a book which has been so long in the possession of mankind should contain many truths as yet undiscovered."
~ *Bishop Butler, English Theologian, Philosopher, 1692-1752*

"Then you will know the Truth, and the Truth will set you free."
~ *John 8:32 NIV*

Thank You for:

436. _____

437. _____

438. _____

Thank You 1095
May 27

"I am thankful to have learned to distinguish between ownership and possession. Books, music, pictures and all the beautiful things of this world belong to those who understand them; we own them by divine right. So I care not a bit who possesses more than I, for I own all the beauty I choose to carry with me."
~ *Author Unknown*

"Glad that I live am I, that the sky is blue; Glad for the country lanes, and the fall of dew; After the sun, the rain, after the rain, then sun; This is the way of life, till the work is done; All that we need to do, be we low or high, is to see that we grow, nearer to the sky."
~ *Lizette Woodworth Reese, American Teacher, Poet, 1856-1935*

Thank You for:

439. _____

440. _____

441. _____

Thank You 1095
May 28

"A very little boy wanted to remove a very large rock from his sandbox. With a great deal of struggle he pushed against the rock with his feet and slowly moved it to the edge of the sandbox. With all his might he tried to shove the rock over the edge of the box, but could not. He worked for a very long time, but the rock would not budge. Completely worn out, the little boy finally sat back on his haunches and began to cry.

His father, who had been watching from a window, came into the yard. "My son why didn't you use all your strength?" he asked. The little boy sobbed, "But daddy, I did!" The father smiled. "No my son, not all your strength; you didn't ask for my help." With that, he reached into the sandbox and easily lifted out the rock. Then he picked up his son, wiped away his tears, and set him back into the box, a little wiser and at peace, to resume his play."
~ Author Unknown

Thank You for:

442. _____

443. _____

444. _____

Thank You 1095
May 29

"Life has loveliness to sell, all beautiful and splendid things, blue waves whitened on a cliff, soaring fire that sways and sings, and children's faces looking up, holding wonder like a cup. "
~ *Sara Teasdale, American Poet, 1884-1933*

"Take time to notice and be thankful. The world will wait while you show the child the rainbow, and teach him how to say thanks, but the rainbow won't wait until you are done working."
~ *Author Unknown*

"A thing of beauty is a joy forever. Its loveliness increases; it will never pass into nothingness."
~ *John Keats, English Romantic Poet, 1795-1821*

Thank You for:

445. _____

446. _____

447. _____

Thank You 1095
May 30

"Think on the men and women who some were born into poverty, sickness and prejudice, who faced and endured pain, imprisonment, disappointment and impossible odds, who never gave up, who changed our world.

Learn from their lives; be thankful for the benefits we have because of them; and be thankful that you and I have the same choices, the same potential as Rosa Parks, Joan of Arc, Abraham Lincoln, Florence Nightingale, Martin Luther, Helen Keller, Martin Luther King, Joni Eareckson Tada, Albert Einstein, Marie Curie, Jesse Owens, Ludwig von Beethoven, Anne Frank, William Tyndale, Harriet Tubman, Nelson Mandela, the list goes on; the possibilities still go on as long as there are those of us who are willing to be thankful, and brave, and to believe that God is bigger than our circumstances, bigger than ourselves."
~ *Connie Ruth Christiansen*

Thank You for:

448. _____

449. _____

450. _____

Thank You 1095
May 31

"The sun does not shine for a few trees and flowers, but for the wide world's joy."
~ *Henry Ward Beecher, Clergyman, Social Reformer, Abolitionist, 1813-1887*

"Look at the flowers, for no reason. It is simply unbelievable how happy flowers are."
~ *Ancient Japanese Philosophy*

"Let the fields be jubilant, and everything in them. Then all the trees of the forest will sing for joy."
~ *Psalm 96:12 NIV*

"A few minutes ago every tree was excited, bowing to the roaring storm, waving, swirling, tossing their branches in glorious enthusiasm like worship. But though to the outer ear these trees are now silent, their songs never cease."
~ *John Muir, Scottish-American Author, Naturalist, 1838-1914*

Thank You for:

451. _____

452. _____

453. _____

Thank You 1095
June 1

"Thanksgiving is a good thing. Thanks-living is better."
~ *Author Unknown*

"Give to your enemy forgiveness, to your opponent tolerance, to a friend your heart, to your customer service, to all men charity, to every child a good example, to your parents' honor, to your spouse devotion, to your self respect; and to your God give thanksgiving for: your enemy, your opponent, your friend, your family, your customer, your opportunities, your life."
~ *Author Unknown*

Thank You for:

454. _____

455. _____

456. _____

Thank You 1095
June 2

"What we are when we are born is God's gift to us. What we become is our gift to God."
~ Author Unknown

"Down to the last detail we are all uniquely different. Recognize and rejoice in that endless variety. The white light of the divine purpose streams down from heaven to be broken up by these human prisms into all the colors of the rainbows. Take your own color in the pattern and be just that."
~ Charles R. Brown, American Novelist, Historian, Editor, 1777-1810

"To accept and to live who God created you to be, is gratitude."
~ Connie Ruth Christiansen

Thank You for:

457. _____

458. _____

459. _____

Thank You 1095
June 3

"Fun is a state of mind."
~ Author Unknown

"Balloons, Yo-Yos, building-blocks, jacks; pick-up-sticks, dice, playing cards, bats; balls, hula-hoops, Frisbees, clay; dolls, teddy bears, trucks, piggy banks; little yellow ducks in a bathtub full of bubbles, and blowing bubbles from a wand; memories or still playing with them now, thank You for toys that cheer us up."
~ Connie Ruth Christiansen

"One joy shatters a hundred griefs."
~ Ancient Chinese Proverb

Thank You for:

460. _____

461. _____

462. _____

Thank You 1095
June 4

"To educate yourself for the feeling of gratitude means to take nothing for granted, but to always seek out and value the kind that will stand behind the action.

Nothing that is done for you is simply a matter of course. Everything originates in a will for the good, which is directed at you. Train yourself never to put off the word or action that is an expression of gratitude."
~ *Albert Schweitzer, Franco-German Theologian, Organist, Philosopher, Physician, 1875-1965*

"Every day may not seem good, but there is something good in every day."
~ *Author Unknown*

Thank You for:

463. _____

464. _____

465. _____

Thank You 1095
June 5

"When you arise in the morning, think of what a precious privilege it is to be alive."
~ *Marcus Aurelius, Roman Emperor, Philosopher, 121-180*

"If the sight of the blue skies fills you with joy, if a blade of grass springing up in the fields has power to move you, if the simple things in nature have a message you understand, rejoice, for your soul is alive."
~ *Eleanora Duse, Italian Actress, 1858-1924*

"All that we need to make us really happy is something to be enthusiastic about."
~ *Charles Kingsley, English Clergyman, Professor, Historian, Novelist, 1819-1875*

Thank You for:

466. _____

467. _____

468. _____

Thank You 1095
June 6

"Walking alone with my dog, in the late morning, in the woods, I started to sing, as I often do. I lifted my thoughts heavenward and sang with great flare. And there, to a tree limb just above my head came a tiny bird, and then another, and another. They landed one, two, three in a row onto a brown leafless branch. With heads all tilted in unison to the right, their dark eyes twinkling, smiling at me, they sat perfectly still as I sounded my praise.

When the song came to an elaborate end, they each cocked their heads to the left, and then again to the right. One chirped, then another, then the other. And then one by one they flittered quickly away.

Delighted, I stood pondering why these creatures made of feathers and music would want to listen to me. I think perhaps they too were out and about enjoying the day; were passing by; heard and recognized the sounds of worship, and simply stopped to agree with me in prayer."
~ *Connie Ruth Christiansen*

Thank You for:

469. _____

470. _____

471. _____

Thank You 1095
June 7

"Life itself won't give you joy unless you really will it. Life just gives you time and space it's up to you to fill it. Learn to make the most of life, lose no happy day. Time can never bring you back chances swept away.

Leave no tender word unsaid, love while life shall last. The mill will never turn again, with water that has past."
~ *Author Unknown*

"I endeavor to be wise when I cannot be merry, easy when I cannot be glad, content with what cannot be mended, and patient when there be no redress."
~ *Elizabeth Montagu, Social Reformer, Literary Critic, Writer, 1718-1800*

Thank You for:

472. _____

473. _____

474. _____

Thank You 1095
June 8

"Be thankful that it is possible to make a difference."
~ *Author Unknown*

"Lord, make me an instrument of your peace. Where there is hatred, let me sow love; where there is injury, pardon; where there is doubt, faith; where there is despair, hope; where there is darkness, light; where there is sadness, joy. O Divine Master, grant that I may not so much seek to be consoled as to console; to be understood as to understand; to be loved as to love. For it is in giving that we receive; it is in pardoning that we are pardoned; and it is in dying that we are born to eternal life."
~ *St. Francis of Assisi, Catholic Preacher, Founder of the Franciscan Monks, 1182-1226*

Thank You for:

475. _____

476. _____

477. _____

Thank You 1095
June 9

"Contentment is not the fulfillment of what you want, but a life of thanksgiving for what you already have."
~ Author Unknown

"Contentment is a pearl of great price and whoever procures it at the expense of ten thousand desires makes a wise and happy purchase."
~ John Balguy, English Theologian, Philosopher, 1686-1738

"True contentment is a real, even an active virtue; affirmative and creative. It's the power of getting out of any situation all there is in it."
~ Gilbert K. Chesterton, British Theologian, Poet, Playwright, Journalist, 1874-1936

Thank You for:

478. _____

479. _____

480. _____

Thank You 1095
June 10

"Before you think of speaking an unkind word, think of someone who can't speak; Before you are irritated with the noise, think of someone who can't hear; Before you complain about the taste of your food, think of someone who has nothing to eat; Before you criticize your husband or wife, think of someone who is crying out for a companion; Before you grumble about your children, think of someone who desires children but they are barren; Before you protest about a house to clean, think of people who are living on the streets; Before you whine about your job, think of the unemployed and disabled who have no job; Before you condemn another, think of your own shortcomings; Before you gripe about your life, think of the one who was taken from this life too soon; Before you are discontent, be thankful."
~ Author Unknown

Thank You for:

481. _____

482. _____

483. _____

Thank You 1095
June 11

"What we call the beginning is often the end. And to make an end is to make a beginning. The end is where we start from."
~ T.S. Eliot, British American Playwright, Literary Critic, Poet, 1888-1965

"If there is a future there is time for mending; time to see your troubles come to an ending. Life is never hopeless however great your sorrow, if you're looking forward to a new tomorrow.
If there is time for wishing then there is time for hoping, when through doubt and darkness you are blindly groping. Though the heart be heavy and hurt you may be feeling, if there is time for praying, there is time for healing.
So if through your window there is a new day breaking, thank God for the promise, though mind and soul be aching. If with harvest over there is grain enough for gleaning, there is a new tomorrow and life still has meaning."
~ Author Unknown

Thank You for:

484. _____

485. _____

486. _____

Thank You 1095
June 12

"Trials, temptations, disappointments; all these are helps instead of hindrances, if one uses them rightly. They not only test the fiber of character but strengthen it. Every conquering temptation represents a new fund of moral energy. Every trial endured and weathered in the right spirit makes a soul nobler and stronger."
~ *James Buckham, AKA Paul Pastnor, American Poet, Professor, Journalist, 1959-1908*

"My strength is made perfect in weakness."
~ *2 Corinthians 12:10b NKJV*

"The brave man is not he who does not feel afraid, but he who conquers that fear."
~ *Nelson Mandela, contemporary South African President, Anti-Apartheid Activist, Nobel Peace Prize recipient, 1918-*

Thank You for:

487. _____

488. _____

489. _____

Thank You 1095
June 13

"Seek the awesome, and when you are awed, give thanks to our Creator."
~ Author Unknown

"The most beautiful system of the sun, planets, and comets, could only proceed from the counsel and dominion of an Intelligent and powerful Being."
~ Isaac Newton, British Physicist who introduced us to gravity, 1642-1727

"The holiness of God is everywhere present; the holiness of the Godhead is conveyed by the holiness of symbols.'"
~ Max Planck, German Physicist who introduced us to quantum physics, 1858-1947

Thank You for:

490. _____

491. _____

492. _____

Thank You 1095
June 14

"He chose to build us from the dirt, to plant us in this garden -- His love compelled Him. Grateful hearts are compelled to love in return."
~ *Connie Ruth Christiansen*

"We love Him because He first loved us."
~ *John 4:19 KJV*

"Love the Lord with all your heart, and with all your soul, and with all your mind. Love your neighbor as yourself."
~ *Matthew 22:37b, 39b NKJV*

Thank You for:

493. _____

494. _____

495. _____

Thank You 1095
June 15

"*God is* a Father to the fatherless."
~ *Psalm 68:5a NKJV*

""Me, me, daddy, look at me, look at me!" The familiar cry of many a child. And many a child's cry has gone unnoticed. Our earthly fathers, even those who are good and kind, are not everything we need. God steps in and is the Father we crave. He looks, He sees, He hears the child; the adult-child say "Daddy, look at me!" He responds well; sometimes through the actions of another, and sometimes by cradling His child in Arms of beyond-our-understanding Otherworld comfort."
~ *Connie Ruth Christiansen*

Thank You for:

496. _____

497. _____

498. _____

Thank You 1095
June 16

"Keep on sowing your seed, for you never know which will grow – perhaps it all will."
~ *Albert Einstein, Physicist, Philosopher, Winner of the Nobel Prize, 1879-1936*

"Plant a thought, reap an act; plant an act, reap a habit; plant a habit, reap a character; plant a character, reap a destiny, plant a gratitude, reap a joy."
~ *Author Unknown*

"A man reaps what he sows."
~ *Galatians 6:7 NIV*

Thank You for:

499. _____

500. _____

501. _____

Thank You 1095
June 17

"Every tomorrow has a set of two handles. We can take hold of it by the handles of anxiety and doubt, or by the handles of thanksgiving and faith."
~ *Author Unknown*

"Don't dwell on what might have been or the chances you have missed. Or the lonely nights that lie between the last time lovers kissed. Don't grasp too hard the memory of the things that never came, the door that did not open or the wind that killed the flame. There is still time enough to live; today, and time enough to try again. Be thankful. Be happy."
~ *Author Unknown*

Thank You for:

502. _____

503. _____

504. _____

Thank You 1095
June 18

"A grateful mind is both a great and a fully happy mind."
~ Author Unknown

"Haven't got a lot of riches, and sometimes the going's tough. But I've got loving ones all around me, and that makes me rich enough. I thank God for his blessings, and the mercies He's bestowed. I'm drinking from my saucer, because my cup has overflowed.

If God gives me strength and courage, when the way grows steep and rough, I'll not ask for other blessings, I'm already blessed enough. And may I never be too busy to help others bear their loads. I'll keep drinking from my saucer, because my cup has overflowed."
~ Author Unknown

Thank You for:

505. _____

506. _____

507. _____

Thank You 1095
June 19

"All Scripture is inspired by God and is useful to teach us."
~ 2 Timothy 3:16 NLT

"He chose fishermen to teach us of storms and peace, a tax collector to teach us of hoarding and giving, family members to remind us that our gifts and calling are independent of our family support, a doubter to show us that faith is greater, a zealot, a put-my-foot-in-my-mouth-often person, a prostitute, a legalist, a bungler.

I am thankful for His choice of disciples; the men and women He called friends here on earth. Their personalities and occupations remind us of ourselves, and that no one is beyond redemption, and that God can and does appreciate and utilize the ordinary, the ugly and the awkward in each of us."
~ Connie Ruth Christiansen

Thank You for:

508. _____

509. _____

510. _____

Thank You 1095
June 20

"The grateful mind is constantly fixed upon the best. Therefore it tends to become the best. It takes the form or character of the best, and will receive the best."
~ *Wallace D. Wattles, Author of Self-Help and Prosperity books, 1860-1911*

"Thankfulness removes the rust from the mind, lubricates our inward machinery, and enables us to do our work with fewer creaks and groans. It has the power to change a community, to promote health and morality, change attitudes, change situations, and change us! Thankful people live longest here on earth, and afterward in our hearts."
~ *Author Unknown*

Thank You for:

511. _____

512. _____

513. _____

Thank You 1095
June 21

"Life around us, things of nature, birth, death are held up as a mirror so we can see more clearly, and be thankful for the metamorphoses of our lives."
~ Author Unknown

"She prayed every day, upon waking and sleeping, working and waiting, she did not stop, time went by and it seemed that God was not listening, doubting and trusting questions why and believing, then she died and there in the Presence of all wisdom, all knowing, her queries were contented, her fears were no more, her dying produced occasions that brought about answers she had so long sought for.

Be it death of a seed, a dream, or the body, life as we know it requires a dying. The ending of one brings life to the other."
~ Connie Ruth Christiansen

Thank You for:

514. _____

515. _____

516. _____

Thank You 1095
June 22

"Pride slays thanksgiving, but a humble mind is the soil out of which thanks naturally grows."
~ *Henry Ward Beecher, American Minister, 1813-1887*

"By humility and the fear of the Lord are riches, and honor, and life."
~ *Proverbs 22:4 NKJV*

"Humility is wisdom. Humility is a certain defense against humiliation."
~ *Author Unknown*

Thank You for:

517. _____

518. _____

519. _____

Thank You 1095
June 23

"Curiosity has its own reason for existing. One cannot help but be in awe when he contemplates the mysteries of eternity, of life, of the marvelous structure of reality. It is enough if one tries merely to comprehend a little of this mystery every day. Never lose a holy curiosity."
~ *Albert Einstein, Physicist, Philosopher, Winner of the Nobel Prize, 1879-1936*

"A wonderful fact to reflect upon, that every human creature is constituted to be that profound secret and mystery to every other."
~ *Charles Dickens, Author of Oliver Twist, A Christmas Carol, and Great Expectations, 1812-1870*

Thank You for:

520. _____

521. _____

522. _____

Thank You 1095
June 24

"Are not five sparrows sold for two cents? Yet not one of them is forgotten before God. You are worth more."
~ *Luke 12:6 NASB*

"Why should I feel discouraged, why should the shadows come; Why should my heart be lonely and long for heaven and home? When Jesus is my portion, my constant friend is He; His eye is on the sparrow and I know He watches me.

Whenever I am tempted, whenever clouds arise; when song gives place to sighing, when hope within me dies; I draw the closer to Him, for care He sets me free, His eye is on the sparrow, and I know He watches me."
~ *Hymn written in 1905 by Civilla Martin, 1866-1948*

Thank You for:

523. _____

524. _____

525. _____

Thank You 1095
June 25

"Be glad of life because it gives you the chance to love and to work and to play, and to look at the stars; to be satisfied with your possessions but not content with yourself until you have made the best of them; to despise nothing in the world except falsehood and meanness, and to fear nothing except cowardice; to be governed by your admirations rather than by your disgusts; to covet nothing that is your neighbors except his kindness of heart and gentleness of manners; to think seldom of your enemies, often of your friends, and every day of Christ; to spend as much time as you can in God's out-of-doors."
   ~ Henry Van Dyke, American Author, Educator, Clergyman, 1852-1933

Thank You for:

526. _____

527. _____

528. _____

Thank You 1095
June 26

"An early morning walk is a blessing for the whole day."
~ Author Unknown

"Climb the mountains and get their good tidings. Nature's peace will flow into you as sunshine flows into trees. The winds will blow their own freshness into you, and the storms their energy, while cares will drop off like autumn leaves."
~ John Muir, Scottish-American Author, Naturalist, 1838-1914

"I will wake the dawn with my song."
~ Psalm 57:8b NLT

Thank You for:

529. _____

530. _____

531. _____

Thank You 1095
June 27

"Pleasure is spread through the earth in stray gifts to be claimed by whoever shall find."
   ~ William Wordsworth, English Romantic Poet, 1770-1850

"You never know when someone might catch a dream from you. Or something you say may open up the windows of a mind that seeks light; the way you live may not matter at all, but you never know, it might.

And just in case it could be that another's life, through you, might possibly change for the better with a brighter view, it seems it might be worth a try at pointing the way to the right.

Of course it may not matter at all that you were thankful and kind, but then again, it might."
   ~ Author Unknown

Thank You for:

532. _____

533. _____

534. _____

Thank You 1095
June 28

"Little wonders are continually around us. But if we don't notice that wonderfulness, we may be tempted to think of our days as monotonous; as grey. A grateful heart will brighten that grey.

And then there are those moments when the wonderfulness is so very obvious, we are so busy enjoying, we may forget to give thanks: The receipt of a gift, the birth of a child; walking down the aisle in white, walking down the aisle in cap and gown; winning a race, finishing a daunting task; a new job, a new friend, a new baby, a new bike; a first kiss, a first home, the first time we realize we have created something truly unique.

For the subtle hues of our days, and for the moments that color life vibrant, thank You."

~ Connie Ruth Christiansen

Thank You for:

535. _____

536. _____

537. _____

Thank You 1095
June 29

"Stop every now and then. Just stop and enjoy. Take a deep breath. Relax and take in the abundance of life."
~ *Author Unknown*

"Rest is not idleness, and to lie sometimes on the grass under trees on a summer's day, listening to the murmur of the water, or watching the clouds float across the sky, is by no means a waste of time."
~ *John Lubbock, renowned Archeologist, Biologist, Politician, 1834-1913*

"Certain thoughts are prayers. There are moments when whatever the attitude of the body, the soul is on its knees."
~ *Victor Hugo, French Writer, Poet, Human Rights Activist, Statesman, 1802-1885*

Thank You for:

538. _____

539. _____

540. _____

Thank You 1095
June 30

"Happiness does not consist of things, but in the relish we have of them."
~ Francois duc de la Rochefoucaid, French Catholic Cardinal, 1558-1645

"A table, a chair, a bowl of fruit and a violin; what else does a man need to be happy?"
~ Albert Einstein, Physicist, Philosopher, Winner of the Nobel Prize, 1879-1936

"Happiness is a grateful spirit, an optimistic attitude, and a heart full of love."
~ Author Unknown

Thank You for:

541. _____

542. _____

543. _____

Thank You 1095
July 1

"This day I will walk beside a sparkling stream that winds its way into the quiet wood, reflecting in its depth a passing cloud...on grassy banks find peace and quietude.

This day I will take a path down to the shore on silver sand. I will walk beside the sea to feel the sea-washed air upon my face, as white-capped waves roll in to welcome me.

This day I will see in all this beauty near, the peace and joy that nature seems to give. The morning sun will find a thankful heart, that in this glory God will let me live."
~ *Author Unknown*

Thank You for:

544. _____

545. _____

546. _____

Thank You 1095
July 2

"Take full account of the excellencies which you possess, and in gratitude remember how you would hanker after them, if you had them not."
~ Marcus Aurelius, Roman Emperor, Philosopher, 121-180

"Bring to memory family, friends, and strangers whose words or actions have made you smile, made you laugh, calmed your troubled soul, lifted your spirits, healed your hurt, filled your mind with possibilities, spurred you on to hope and greater accomplishments; those who have appreciated you, accepted you, loved you.
Be thankful for these gift givers that come and go, offering bits and pieces of their excellent selves to you."
~ Connie Ruth Christiansen

Thank You for:

547. _____

548. _____

549. _____

Thank You 1095
July 3

"For cars and trucks and trains, buses, trolleys, shuttles and planes;

For roller skates, ice skates and bikes, skis inner tubes, and trikes

For wagons, sleds and snowboards, buggies strollers and skateboards;

For horses, mules and carts, carriages wheelbarrows and flatcars;

For stairways, winches and cranes; scaffolds, pulleys and cranes,

For crutches and wheelchairs, orthotics and braces, sidewalks, ramps and streets;

For legs and feet, and for all the things that help get us to where we are going;

Thank You."

~ Connie Ruth Christiansen

Thank You for:

550. _____

551. _____

552. _____

Thank You 1095
July 4

"I have lived a long time, and the longer I live, the more convincing proofs I see of this truth: That God governs the affairs of men. And if a tiny bird cannot fall to the ground without His notice, it is probably that an empire cannot rise without His aid. We have been assured, in the sacred writings that "except the Lord build the house, they labor in vain who build it.""
   ~ Benjamin Franklin, U. S. Founding Father, Civic Activist, Statesman, Diplomat, Inventor, 1706-1790

"Give thanks to the Supreme Ruler of the Universe for the inestimable civil and religious blessings with which we are favored."
   ~ James K. Polk, 11th President of the United States, 1795-1849

Thank You for:

553. _____

554. _____

555. _____

Thank You 1095
July 5

"There are crucial moments when the will of a handful of free men of faith breaks through determinism and opens up new roads."
~ Charles de Gaulle, French WWII Statesman, General, President, 1890-1970

"When a brave man takes a stand, the spines of others are often stiffened."
~ Billy Graham, Evangelist, Author, Spiritual Counselor to several U.S. Presidents, 1918-

"I am thankful that in taking the risk of making a stand, I always come out ahead -- If I win, I am happy; if I lose I am wiser."
~ Author Unknown

Thank You for:

556. _____

557. _____

558. _____

Thank You 1095
July 6

"There is a law of gratitude, and it is this: the natural principle that action and reaction are always equal and in opposite directions.

The grateful outreaching of your mind in thankful praise to Supreme Intelligence is a liberation or expenditure of force. It cannot fail to reach that to which it is addressed, and the reaction is an instantaneous movement toward you.

But the value of gratitude does not consist solely in getting you more blessings in the future. Without gratitude you cannot long keep from dissatisfied thoughts regarding things as they are."
~ *Wallace D. Wattles, Author of Self-Help and Prosperity books, 1860-1911*

"Live in rooms full of light."
~ *Aurelius Cornelius Celsus, Roman-Latin Author, 25 BC -14 A D*

Thank You for:

559. _____

560. _____

561. _____

Thank You 1095
July 7

"A young boy and his father were walking on the mountains. Suddenly the boy fell, hurt himself, and screamed, "Ahhhhh!" To his surprise, he heard a voice in the distance repeating his "Ahhhhh!" Curious, he called out, "Who are you?" He received this answer: "Who are you?" Angered at the response the boy hollered back, "Coward!" The reply came: "Coward!"

Frustrated, the boy looked up to see his father smiling. The father cupped his hands to his mouth. "I admire you!" He hollered. "I admire you!" was the reply. "Thank you!" The father called out. "Thank you!" The voice responded.

The little boy was delighted but did not understand. And so the father explained about echoes. And then he said: "An echo teaches us about life. Echoes repeat back everything you say. So does life -- Your life will be an echo of your words.""

~ Author Unknown

Thank You for:

562. _____

563. _____

564. _____

Thank You 1095
July 8

"A vacation is like being in love – it is anticipated with pleasure, experienced with some discomfort and remembered with nostalgia."
~ *Author Unknown*

"For planning and waiting, for anticipation and packing, for getting away, for doing something new, for fresh sights and sounds and smells, for storing up memories, for being tired from resting, for wanting home again, for coming home again, for a home to leave and come back to, thank You."
~ *Connie Ruth Christiansen*

Thank You for:

565. _____

566. _____

567. _____

Thank You 1095
July 9

"There was a large pile of stones ready for use, and there was a job to be done. Not a very difficult job, but a necessary one.

Several capable people stood nearby the pile of stones. Their names were Everybody, Somebody, Anybody, Nobody and Thankful.

Everybody was sure that Somebody would do the job. Anybody could have done it well but Nobody did it at all. Somebody got angry with that, because it was Everybody's job. Everybody thought Anybody should do it, but Nobody seem to realize that Everybody wouldn't do it.

It ended up that Everybody blamed Somebody when Nobody did what Anybody could have done.

Then Thankful picked up a stone and handed it to Somebody, and the work began. Soon Everybody joined Somebody and Nobody any longer blamed Anybody."
~ *Author Unknown*

Thank You for:

568. _____

569. _____

570. _____

Thank You 1095
July 10

"A gem cannot be polished without friction, nor a man perfected without trials."
~ Ancient Chinese Proverb

"All sunny skies would be too bright; All morning hours mean too much light; All laughing days too much a strain; There must be clouds, and night, and rain, and shut-in days, to make us see the beauty of life's tapestry."
~ Author Unknown

"We must pass through the darkness, to reach the light."
~ Albert Pike, American Lawyer, Journalist, Soldier, 1809-1891

Thank You for:

571. _____

572. _____

573. _____

Thank You 1095
July 11

"God is a circle whose center is everywhere and circumference nowhere."
~ Timaeus of Locris, 5th Century BC Greek Philosopher

"He is far beyond our comprehension. And yet, He makes Himself understood in a very personal way; He allows us to see bits and pieces of Himself and to experience a portion of His presence. He involves Himself in our lives. He speaks to us, listens to us. He is above us to oversee, before us to guide, behind us to protect, beside us to comfort, within us to empower."
~ Connie Ruth Christiansen

"Just as there comes a warm sunbeam into every cottage window, so comes a love born of God's care for every separate need."
~ Author Unknown

Thank You for:

574. _____

575. _____

576. _____

Thank You 1095
July 12

"Lessons From Noah's Ark:

Plan Ahead -- It wasn't raining while he was building the ark.

Don't Listen to Critics – Just keep doing what you know has to be done.

Travel in Pairs – Two heads are often better than one, and safer.

Speed Isn't Always an Advantage – Yes, cheetahs got on board, but so did the snails.

Take Care -- of your animals and family, as if they were the last ones on earth.

Remember -- The woodpeckers inside are often a bigger threat than the storm outside.

Believe – No matter how bleak it looks there is a rainbow on the other side.

Be Thankful – For high ground, for shelter, and for second chances."

~ Author Unknown

Thank You for:

577. _____

578. _____

579. _____

Thank You 1095
July 13

"The 7-ups:
Wake up – Decide to have a good day
Dress up – A smile is the best accessory
Shut up – Listen more than you speak
Stand up – For what you believe in
Look up – To the mercy and grace of God
Reach up – For something higher
Lift up – Your prayer of thanksgiving."
~ Author Unknown

"Give thanks to the Lord, for He is good."
~ Psalm 118:29 KJV

Thank You for:

580. _____

581. _____

582. _____

Thank You 1095
July 14

"Early morning, a cup of tea, the others are sleeping. Sit at the table, Bible before me, sun through the window. A bird just outside on a branch getting ready to sing, but quiet for now; everything is quiet for now. Soak in the rays and the words from the Book; drink in the quiet, the peace, the tea. Thankful, prepare for the day.

Late in the evening, rise from my knees, the others are sleeping. Climb into the bed, head soft on a pillow, the weight of the covers. No other sound but that of my breathing; a soft drowsy calm. Soak in the peace, wait for the dreams. Thankful, let go of the day."
~ *Connie Ruth Christiansen*

Thank You for:

583. _____

584. _____

585. _____

Thank You 1095
July 15

"An eagle knows when a storm is approaching long before it breaks. He will fly to some high spot and wait for the winds to come. When the storm hits, the eagle sets its wings so that the wind will pick him up and lift him above the storm. While the storm rages below, the eagle is soaring above it. He does not escape the storm; he simply uses the storm to fly higher. He rises on the winds that bring the storm.

When the storms of life come, and we can see them coming because they always come; expect them to come, we can rise above them by setting our minds on Him; setting our minds on thankfulness, faith, hope, so that the wind of God will pick us up and lift us above the storms.

Be thankful that in the end it is not the storms of life that will weigh us down, it is where we set our focus; where we set our wings."
~ *Author Unknown*

Thank You for:

586. _____

587. _____

588. _____

Thank You 1095
July 16

"For playhouses, tree houses, and trees to climb; For tire swings, and playground swings, and swinging on a vine; For swinging a bat, and hitting a ball, running the bases, hearing the call of the crowd; For cheering and clapping and jumping with glee; For reasons to celebrate, thank You."
~ Connie Ruth Christiansen

"Never condemn yourself to a life without cause to celebrate and be thankful. Never forget the people you love and love them when you have an occasion to do so. Celebrate their life and celebrate your own."
~ Author Unknown

Thank You for:

589. _____

590. _____

591. _____

Thank You 1095
July 17

"Life is beauty, admire it.
Life is bliss, taste it.
Life is a dream, realize it.
Life is a challenge, meet it.
Life is a duty, complete it.
Life is a game, play it.
Life is a promise, fulfil it.
Life is sorrow, overcome it.
Life is a song, sing it.
Life is a struggle, accept it.
Life is a tragedy, confront it.
Life is an adventure, dare it.
Life is luck, make it.
Life is too precious, do not destroy it.
Life is life, fight for it.
Life is an opportunity, benefit from it."
~ Mother Teresa, Catholic Nun, Missionary, Nobel Peace Prize winner, 1910-1997

Thank You for:

592. _____

593. _____

594. _____

Thank You 1095
July 18

"Some men see things as they are and say "why?" I dream things that never were and say "why not?""
~ *Robert Francis Kennedy, Civil Rights Activist, U.S. Senator, Attorney General, 1925-1968*

"If He could do those wonders then, let us prove our mighty God again. Why can't the God who raised the dead, gave little David Goliath's head; cast out the demons with a word, yet sees the fall of one small bird; do signs and miracles today. He can! He is just the same today."
~ *Martin Luther, German Priest who initiated the Protestant Reformation, 1483-1546*

Thank You for:

595. _____

596. _____

597. _____

Thank You 1095
July 19

"Some days thanksgiving surges up from the center of me and spills over, out of my actions, my mouth. Other days it is but an act of my will. "I will be grateful today," I say. "I will look for the silver lining in the cloud that is hanging over me. No matter the circumstances, I will find something, many things to be thankful for." And as I go my way determined, my act of will becomes what I feel and once again thanksgiving surges up from the center of me and spills over."
~ *Connie Ruth Christiansen*

"Electricity and gratitude are much the same in that they must be continually charged up and used up in order to exist."
~ *Author Unknown*

Thank You for:

598. _____

599. _____

600. _____

Thank You 1095
July 20

"Look around you, breathe in beauty; look up, breathe out thanksgiving."
   ~ Connie Ruth Christiansen

"As for me, I know nothing else but miracles. Whether I walk the streets of Manhattan, or dart my sight over the roofs of houses towards the sky, or wade with naked feet along the beach just in the edge of the water, or stand under the trees in the woods, or talk by day with any one I love, or sleep in bed at night with any one I love, or watch honey bees busy around the hive of a summer forenoon, or the wonderfulness of the sundown, or of the stars shining so quiet and bright, or the exquisite delicate thin curve of the new moon in spring..."
   ~ Walt Whitman, American Poet, Essayist, Journalist, 1819-1892

Thank You for:

   601. _____

   602. _____

   603. _____

Thank You 1095
July 21

"It is only a tiny rosebud, a flower of God's design, but I cannot unfold the petals with these clumsy hands of mine; the secret of unfolding flowers is not known to such as I. God opens flowers so sweetly when in my hand they but fade and die.

If I cannot unfold the rosebud this flower of God's design, then how do I think I have the wisdom to unfold this life of mine? So I'll trust Him for His leading each moment of the day; I will look to Him for guidance each step along the way.

The pathway, which lies before me, only the Heavenly Father knows. I will trust in Him to unfold the moments and the mystery, just as He unfolds the rose."
~ *Author Unknown*

Thank You for:

604. _____

605. _____

606. _____

Thank You 1095
July 22

"You will never have it all together so remember: success stops when you stop.

Others can stop you temporarily but no one can ruin your day or your life without your permission.

The best way to escape your problem is to work through it and solve it – look for opportunities, not guarantees.

We often fear doing the thing we want the most, but if we don't start, it is certain we will not arrive.

We may run, walk, stumble, drive, or fly, but let us never lose sight of the reason for the journey.

And never miss a chance to be thankful for beauty along the way."
~ *Author Unknown*

Thank You for:

607. _____

608. _____

609. _____

Thank You 1095
July 23

"Good humor is a tonic for mind and body. It is the best antidote for anxiety and depression. It is a business asset. It attracts and keeps friends. It lightens human burdens."
~ *Greenville Kleiser, American Author, 1868-1935*

"Humor must have come straight from the heart of God. Just look at the hilarious shapes and forms that some of His animals took on, as He placed them here and there on this garden Earth.

I know that Adam was new and had nothing to compare them to, but I am quite sure that he was in awe of the lion and the eagle, that he wondered at the giraffe and the elephant, and that he chuckled when he first saw the warthog, the hippopotamus and the kangaroo. And I think maybe God was pleased that Adam appreciated the riddle."
~ *Connie Ruth Christiansen*

Thank You for:

610. _____

611. _____

612. _____

Thank You 1095
July 24

"The 9th decade of my life is approaching almost ominously. Not because of age, but because of ailing health, eyes, and ears. The roar of the traffic on the highway passing by the house is not as loud as it used to be; The howl of the coyote is fainter and lonelier; Bees don't buzz as they move from flower to flower; The fiddling of the cricket doesn't fill the balmy summer evenings; And there are no birds in the tree tops singing their songs of Spring.

But I am thankful for the things I can still feel, see, and hear: A delicious delight when great grandchildren give a hug and holler, "I love you grandpa-great;" the joy in the eyes of my grandchildren when they hug me and say "I love you grandpa;" And a special tug of love when my children hug me and ask, "are you ok Dad?" And then there is that intense longing as I think of, and as I hold my wife of 62 years, and that when we look into each other's eyes, I still hear music."

~ *Carl (Bud) Christiansen, 87, Retired Preacher, Musician, Stone Mason; Used by permission*

Thank You for:

613. _____

614. _____

615. _____

Thank You 1095
July 25

"When you are joyous, look deep into your heart and you shall find it is only that which has given you sorrow that is giving you joy."
~ *Khalil Gibran, Lebanese American Poet, Author of The Prophet, 1883-1931*

"Difficulties are opportunities to better things; they are stepping stones to greater experience. Perhaps someday you will be grateful for some temporary trouble."
~ *Author Unknown*

"It is said that in some countries trees grow but will bear no fruit, because there is no winter there."
~ *John Bunyon, English Preacher, Author of Pilgrims Progress, 1628-1688*

Thank You for:

616. _____

617. _____

618. _____

Thank You 1095
July 26

"The joyful people are those who are generous and kind. The miserable people are those who are selfish and unforgiving.

The problem solvers are those whose lives are empowered by faith and optimism. The problem people are those whose lives are drained by doubts, bitterness and pessimism.

The winners are those who learn to be grateful and to take full responsibility for their actions. The losers are those who are ungrateful and blame others for their failures."
~ *Author Unknown*

"Most people are about as happy as they make up their minds to be."
~ *Abraham Lincoln, 16th President of the U.S., 1809-1865*

Thank You for:

619. _____

620. _____

621. _____

Thank You 1095
July 27

"Count your blessings instead of your crosses, your gains instead of your losses. Count your joys instead of your woes and your friends instead of your foes. Count your smiles instead of your tears, your courage instead of your fears. Count your full years instead of your lean, your kind deeds instead of your mean. Count your health instead of your wealth, and count on God instead of yourself."
~ *Author Unknown*

"When upon life's billows you are tempest tossed, when you are discouraged, thinking all is lost, count your many blessings, name them one by one, count your many blessings, see what God has done."
~ *Hymn by Johnson Oatman, Jr., American Pastor who wrote lyrics for more than 3,000 hymns, 1856-1922*

Thank You for:

622. _____

623. _____

624. _____

Thank You 1095
July 28

"The greatest risk in life is to take no risk. To laugh is to risk appearing the fool. To reach out is to risk involvement; To expose feelings is to risk revealing yourself; To love is to risk not being loved in return; To live is to risk dying; To share your ideas is to risk rejection; To hope is to risk despair. To avoid risk, you may temporarily avoid suffering and sorrow, but you will lose more than you gain. The person who risks nothing does nothing, has nothing and becomes nothing."
~ *Author Unknown*

"Thank You for the paradoxes of this earthly existence: that from death comes life; that pain results in joy; that in losing myself I find myself; that careless courage can bring forth careful results; that to serve is to lead; that humility is strength; that in giving I receive."
~ *Connie Ruth Christiansen*

Thank You for:

625. _____

626. _____

627. _____

Thank You 1095
July 29

"Life is a gift that the humblest may boast of, and one that the humblest may well make the most of. Get out and live it each hour of the day, wear it and use it as much as you may. Don't keep it in niches and corners and grooves; you'll find that in service its beauty improves."
~ *Edgar A. Guest, English-American Poet, Journalist, Radio Host, 1881-1959*

"I intend to arrive at the end of this life not in a well-preserved body that has been kept safe for burial but rather to skid in broadside to heaven with a great thanksgiving, totally worn out, and loudly proclaiming, "Wow, thanks for the ride!""
~ *Author Unknown*

Thank You for:

628. _____

629. _____

630. _____

Thank You 1095
July 30

"The goodness of God is seen in the variety of natural pleasures which He has provided for His creatures. God might have been pleased to satisfy our hunger without the food being pleasing to our palates. God has not only given us senses, but also that which gratifies them; and this too reveals His goodness.

The earth might have been fertile without its surface being so delightfully variegated. Our physical lives could have been sustained without beautiful flowers to regale our eyes with their colors, and our nostrils with their sweet perfumes. We might have walked the fields without our ears being saluted by the music of the birds.

Whence then this loveliness, this charm, so freely diffused over the face of nature? Truly, the earth is full of the goodness of the Lord."
~ *Arthur Pink, English Evangelist, Scholar, 1886-1952*

Thank You for:

631. _____

632. _____

633. _____

Thank You 1095
July 31

"Sadness will pass, joy will return. Death will happen, so will birth. Wars will come, thankfully to end. People come and people go. Dreams die and dreams are fulfilled. Life is effort and then it is ease. So goes the wonder that is the bittersweetness of our lives."
~ Connie Ruth Christiansen

"Today I will not imagine what I would do if things were different. They are not different. I will be thankful, and make success with what material I have."
~ Author Unknown

Thank You for:

634. _____

635. _____

636. _____

Thank You 1095
August 1

"Thank You for summer things:
　　For longer days, and sultry nights, for the hot and for the shade;
　　For laundry hanging fresh in the sun, blowing in the breeze;
　　For children smiling as they zoom down a city-park slide;
　　For picnic benches, wading pools, swings and teeter-totters;
　　For snow-cones, and ice-cream truck tunes, and cold lemonade;
　　For sitting on a log watching the ebb and flow of the ocean tide;
　　For the spray of salt-water soft on my skin, seagulls puttering in the sand;
　　For a slower pace, lazy days, and sun-kissed faces."
　　~ Connie Ruth Christiansen

Thank You for:

637. _____

638. _____

639. _____

Thank You 1095
August 2

"Someone here may pass me by, but another stops to turn their eyes in my direction, I make them smile;

Pushing my way through a maze of people seemingly a part of a cog, suddenly face to face, and for a moment at least, a memorable connection;

I sing, I speak, I write and I am but a solitary voice until that one who can relate, finds joy in my reflections;

To one I may seem nothing, but to another I am all;

Thank You that beauty truly is in the eye of the beholder, and that beauty cannot forever go unnoticed."
~ *Connie Ruth Christiansen*

Thank You for:

640. _____

641. _____

642. _____

Thank You 1095
August 3

"I awoke this morning with devout thanksgiving for my friends, the old and new."
~ *Ralph Waldo Emerson, American Philosopher and Poet, 1808-1882*

"I am thankful today for friends. Lifetime friends who have provided the hands and heart of God to me, and new friends that I can discover and learn from. Friendship is a gift."
~ *Cathey Sturtevant, Wife, Mom, Teacher, Life-Coach, Mentor; Used by permission*

"A new friend is as new wine; when it is old, thou shall drink it with pleasure."
~ *Apocrypha, Sirach 9:10*

Thank You for:

643. _____

644. _____

645. _____

Thank You 1095
August 4

"You are my hiding place."
~ *Psalm 32:7 NKJV*

"Be thankful for the times and places you can hide away from the worries of this life, from the weary of the day, from the busy of a job, from the fear of tomorrow, from sorrows of the past.

Be thankful that you can hide away in prayer, in your home, with your family, in a cave from the elements, under a tree from the rain, in the strong arms of a loved one, in a group of friends, in the pages of a good book, in the pictures of a movie, in the company of children, in the companionship of a pet, in music, in exercise, in creativity, in a vacation spot, in your memories, in your dreams."
~ *Connie Ruth Christiansen*

Thank You for:

646. _____

647. _____

648. _____

Thank You 1095
August 5

"It is a delicious moment, certainly, that of being well-nestled in bed and feeling that you shall drop gently to sleep. The good is to come, not past; the limbs are tired enough to render the remaining in one posture delightful; the labor of the day is gone."
~ *R. Leigh Hunt, English Critic, Essayist, Writer, Poet, 1784-1859*

"I am thankful for clean, soft welcoming sheets; a feathery pillow beneath my head; the warm around my limbs, the cool of the night on my face; troubles of the day behind me; joys of the day snug in my heart; happy dreams ahead; a no-guilt time just for me – sleep."
~ *Connie Ruth Christiansen*

Thank You for:

649. _____

650. _____

651. _____

Thank You 1095
August 6

"I am thankful for temperature; for cold, for hot, for warm. How vastly different our lives would be without this variation. I'm grateful for the choices of an ice cold drink of water or a hot cup of tea, or milk just warm enough to help me fall asleep; for very cold ice cream covered with piping hot fudge chocolate; for fresh baked cookies and that they offer a different taste sensation when they are hot, than they do when they've cooled; for piping hot dinners, even better cold the next day for breakfast; for the ice cold of winter snow, the warm of a spring rain and the cool of a wet ocean breeze on a hot summer day; for air conditioners and wood stoves; for fire, for ice, and for all the temperatures in between; thank You for cold, for hot, for warm."
~ Connie Ruth Christiansen

Thank You for:

652. _____

653. _____

654. _____

Thank You 1095
August 7

"Variety is the spice of life."
~Author Unknown

"For Daffodils and Tulips, Roses and Petunias, Snowdrops, Edelweiss, and Balm, Azalea and Begonias;

Baby's breath and Bittersweet, Bluebells and Clematis, Daisies, Elderflower, Yew, Violets and Magnolias;

Mandrake, Zinnia, Witch Hazel, Nettles and Nasturtium, Windfall, Water Flower, Sage, Violet and Wisteria;

Ambrosia, Amaryllis, Aster, Bird of Paradise and Flax, Crocus, Christmas-Rose, and Clover, Galax and Gardenia;

Buttercups and Fuchsia, Filbert and Gloxinia, Goldenrod and Flora's Bell, Goosefoot and Geranium;

Almond Blossom, Apple Blossom, Bachelor Button, Balsam, and for all the many more I don't have room to mention; Thank You!"
~ *Connie Ruth Christiansen*

Thank You for:

655. _____

656. _____

657. _____

Thank You 1095
August 8

"Nature will bear the closest inspection. She invites us to lay our eye level with her smallest leaf, and take an insect view of its plain."
~ *Henry David Thoreau, Author, Poet, Naturalist, Abolitionist, Philosopher, 1817-1862*

"Storm winds rise, gently lifting, wind sings in the trees; Thunder rolls, loudly crashing, wind howls, hearts freeze;
Rain falls smashing, splashing, bright lightning o'er the eves; Clouds dark fiercely rolling, rolling high and far away;
Wind sighs, slowly dying, trees cease tossing like the seas; Water drips softly falling, softly falling on the leaves."
~ *Author Unknown*

Thank You for:

658. _____

659. _____

660. _____

Thank You 1095
August 9

"When people shake their heads because we are living in a restless age, I ask them how they would like to live in a stationary one, and do without change."
~ *George Bernard Shaw, Irish Play-wright, Equal Rights Activist, Economist, 1856-1950*

"When we long for life without difficulties, remind us that oaks grow strong in contrary winds and diamonds are made under pressure."
~ *Peter Marshall, Scottish American Pastor, Husband of Author Catherine Marshall, 1902-1949*

"Thank God even when you don't understand what He is doing."
~ *Author Unknown*

Thank You for:

661. _____

662. _____

663. _____

Thank You 1095
August 10

"The lunatic, the love, and the poet, are of imagination all compact."
~ *William Shakespeare, English Poet, Playwright, 1564- 1616*

"Thank You for the unique, interesting, sometimes a little bit crazy creative minds that put their pen to paper; for the imaginations that give us cartoon characters and knights on white horses who rescue beautiful maidens, and whisk us away to fairy-lands, and up over the other side of rainbows, and challenge us to think outside the box. Thank You for those who are brave enough to share their secret dream-worlds with us."
~ *Connie Ruth Christiansen*

Thank You for:

664. _____

665. _____

666. _____

Thank You 1095
August 11

"Adapt yourself to the things among which your lot has been cast, and love sincerely the fellow creatures with whom destiny has ordained that you shall live."
~ Marcus Aurelius, Roman Emperor, Philosopher, 121-180

"Wake at dawn with a winged heart and give thanks for another day of loving."
~ Khalil Gibran, Lebanese American Artist, Poet, Author of The Prophet, 1883-1931

Thank You for:

667. _____

668. _____

669. _____

Thank You 1095
August 12

"Let me go where'er I will, I hear a sky born music still; It sounds from all things old, it sounds from all things young, from all that's fair, from all that's foul, peals out a cheerful song. Tis not in the high stars alone, nor in the cup of budding flowers, nor in the redbreast's mellow tones, nor in the bow that smiles in showers; but in the mud and scum of things, there always, always, something sings."
  ~ Ralph Waldo Emerson, American Philosopher, Poet, 1808-1882

"As in the rankest soil the most beautiful flowers are grown, so in the dark soil of poverty the choicest flowers of humanity have developed and bloomed."
  ~ James Allen, British Philosopher, Poet, 1868-1912

Thank You for:

670. _____

671. _____

672. _____

Thank You 1095
August 13

"God formed a man from the dust of the ground and breathed into his nostrils the breath of life, and the man became a living being."
~ *Genesis 2:7 NIV*

"When I see an endless ocean touch a boundless sky, finite understanding encounters momentary insight. I have the briefest glimpse of how awesome it all is; the wonder of creation, the magnanimity of Him who by His spoken word gave life to all that is.

In this instant of enlightenment I somehow understand the paradox of how small, and yet significant I am; for it was His decision to create the mortal man not with a verbal statement, but by His gentle hand."
~ *Transitory Illumination, by Connie Ruth Christiansen*

Thank You for:

673. _____

674. _____

675. _____

Thank You 1095
August 14

"There is a legend of an artist who searched a long time for the perfect piece of sandal-wood, out of which to carve a Madonna. He was about to give up in despair, leaving the great vision of his life unrealized, when in a dream he was bidden to shape the figure from a block of plain oak-wood which was destined for the fire. Obeying the command, the artist produced from a common log, a masterpiece.

In like manner many people search for brilliant opportunities to do the beautiful things of which they dream, while the very elements they require for such deeds are close to them in the simplest and most familiar passing events, and in the homeliest of circumstances. They look in vain for perfectly formed resources from which to carve a dream, while common materials waiting to be masterpieces are all around them nearby."

~ J.R. Miller, D.D., American Pastor, Editor, Author, 1840-1912

Thank You for:

676. _____

677. _____

678. _____

Thank You 1095
August 15

"Men achieve a certain greatness unawares, when working to another aim."
~ *Ralph Waldo Emerson, American Philosopher, Poet, 1808-1882*

"Although I may not walk with kings, let me be big in little things. Lord, make me big enough I pray to triumph in a lesser way. When petty disappointments rise, let me be patient, gentle, wise. Missing the joy which greatness brings let me not fail in little things."
~ *Edgar A. Guest, English-American Poet, Journalist, Radio Host, 1881-1959*

"When a man forgets himself, it is then he does something that everyone else remembers."
~ *Author Unknown*

Thank You for:

679. _____

680. _____

681. _____

Thank You 1095
August 16

"The most beautiful people that we know are those who have known defeat, known suffering, known struggle, known loss, and have found their way out of the depths. These persons have an appreciation, a sensitivity, and an understanding of life that fills them with compassion, gentleness, and a deep loving concern. Beautiful people do not just happen."
~ *Elizabeth Kubler-Ross, Swiss Psychiatrist, Author of On Death and Dying, 1926-2004*

"He *makes* everything beautiful in its time."
~ *Ecclesiastes 3:11 paraphrased*

Thank You for:

682. _____

683. _____

684. _____

Thank You 1095
August 17

"Some life-stories, such as that of John Newton (1725-1807) cry out to be repeated again and again, to teach us; to inspire us to believe and to be thankful that evil can indeed be turned around for good, and that forgiveness is offered for even the worst of offenses.

Newton had for many years made his living by capturing, enslaving, beating and selling men, women and children. And then he listened to the Conviction within telling him how wrong was his choice of vocation. He allowed his life to be changed by the truth, and by love. He quit the slave-trade and began instead to speak out boldly against it.

Eventually a song resulted from his forgiven heart, to become one of the most recognized and beloved songs of all time, worldwide:

"Amazing Grace how sweet the sound that saved a wretch like me. I was once was lost but now am found. Was blind but now I see.""
~ *Connie Ruth Christiansen*

Thank You for:

685. _____

686. _____

687. _____

Thank You 1095
August 18

"Walking along a sandy beach, an old man noticed a young man walking ahead of him picking up starfish and throwing them into the sea. The old man asked him, "Why?" The young man replied, "The tide is changing; if I don't throw them in, they will die." Puzzled at the diligence of youth for such a task, the old man said, "Isn't there something better you can do with your time? There are thousands of starfish up and down this beach. You can't possibly make a difference for them all." The young man picked up another starfish and tossed it on to the waves, and said, "But, I did make a difference for that one.""
~ *Author Unknown*

"I am only one, but I am one. I cannot do everything, but I can do something. And I will not let what I cannot do interfere with what I can do."
~ *Edward Everett Hale, American Theologian, Abolitionist, Author, 1822-1902*

Thank You for:

688. _____

689. _____

690. _____

Thank You 1095
August 19

"In ordinary life we hardly realize that we receive a great deal more than we give, and that it is only with gratitude that life becomes rich. It is very easy to overestimate the importance of our own achievements in comparison with what we owe others."
~ *Dietrich Bonhoeffer, German Pastor who was executed by the Nazis for resistance, 1906-1945*

"Remember that what you now have was once among the things only hoped for."
~ *Epictetus, Greek Philosopher, Teacher, 55-135 AD*

Thank You for:

691. _____

692. _____

693. _____

Thank You 1095
August 20

"A limit on what you will do puts a limit on what you can do. Other than that, all things are possible. Thank God for the giants in your life."
~ Author Unknown

"The army of Israel looked at *the giant* Goliath through the eyes of man and said he's too big to beat. David looked at him through the eyes of God and said he's too big to miss."
~ Walter Carter, American Author, 1823-1897

Thank You for:

694. _____

695. _____

696. _____

Thank You 1095
August 21

"When I was a little boy my mother would embroider often. I would sit at her knee and look up from the floor, watching her pull the needle in and out of the fabric within the little round hoop.

From where I sat, what she was doing looked like a jumbled mess, and I would tell her so. She would smile at me and gently say, "My son, come and see it from another side." Climbing on her knee I would be surprised to see a beautiful work of art.

Many times through the years I have looked up to my Heavenly Father and said, "My life looks like a mess to me. It seems so jumbled." And I look forward to the time when I can see it from His side; a work of art."
~ *Author Unknown*

"We are His masterpiece."
~ *Ephesians 2:10 NLT*

Thank You for:

697. _____

698. _____

699. _____

Thank You 1095
August 22

"Watch your thoughts, they become words. Watch your words, they become actions. Watch your actions, they become habits. Watch your habits, they become character. Watch your character, it becomes your destiny."
~ *Author Unknown*

"If you change your thinking around, you will change your words around, if you change your words around, you will change your life around."
~ *Author Unknown*

"Whatever is true, whatever is noble, whatever is right, whatever is pure, whatever is lovely, whatever is admirable, if anything is excellent or praiseworthy, think on such things."
~ *Philippians 4:8 NIV*

Thank You for:

700. _____

701. _____

702. _____

Thank You 1095
August 23

"Rejoice in the Lord always, and again I say rejoice."
~ *Philippians 4:4 KJV*

"I am grateful for what I am and have. My thanksgiving is perpetual. O how I laugh when I think of my vague indefinite riches. No run on my bank can drain it. For my wealth is not possession but enjoyment."
~ *Henry David Thoreau, Author, Poet, Naturalist, Abolitionist, Philosopher 1817-1862*

"Happy moments, praise God; Difficult moment, seek God; Quiet moments, hear God; Painful moments, trust God; Every moment, thank God."
~ *Author Unknown*

Thank You for:

703. _____

704. _____

705. _____

Thank You 1095
August 24

"Dust if you must but wouldn't it be better to paint a picture or write a letter, bake a cake or plant a seed, ponder the difference between what you want and what you need?

Dust if you must but there's not much time with rivers to swim and mountains to climb, music to hear and books to read, friends to cherish and life to lead.

Dust if you must, but the world's out there with the sun in your eyes, the wind in your hair, a flutter of snow, a shower of rain, this day will not come 'round again.

Dust if you must but bear in mind, old age will come and it's not always kind, and when you go and go you must, you yourself will make more dust."

~ *Author Unknown*

Thank You for:

706. _____

707. _____

708. _____

Thank You 1095
August 25

"I will show my joy by sailing sticks across a fresh mud puddle and making a sidewalk with rocks. I will return to a time when life was simple, when all I knew was colors and nursery rhymes. I will be happy; blissfully unaware of all the things that worry and upset. I will show my childlike trust by believing You are fair, that most everyone is honest and good, and that everything is possible. I will be at peace with the complexities of life and be overly excited by minute things. I will play endlessly with my pets and children, make angels in the snow, and let my imagination go on forever. I will live simply again, and believe in the power of smiles, hugs, kind words, truth, justice, peace, and dreams."
~ *Author Unknown*

Thank You for:

709. _____

710. _____

711. _____

Thank You 1095
August 26

"Before I formed you in the womb I knew you… Even to your old age and gray hairs I am He, I am He who will sustain you."
 ~ Jeremiah 1:5a NASB; Isaiah 46:4 NKJV

"For that new baby smell, and that first baby smile; for learning to walk and learning to climb; for trying and growing, for joys and for tears; for all the possibilities of the quick passing years; for wrinkles and wisdom, and changing with time; for moments and memories, and nostalgia that binds; for beginnings, and endings, and for all that is in between; thank You."
 ~ Connie Ruth Christiansen

Thank You for:

712. _____

713. _____

714. _____

Thank You 1095
August 27

"Doubt sees obstacles, faith sees the way."
~ *Author Unknown*

"Obstacles are life. Stop waiting for the obstacles to be gone, Stop waiting until you get a better home, or a better car, until you finish school, or go back to school, until you lose ten pounds, or gain ten pounds, until you have kids, or your kids leave the house, until you start work, until you retire, until you get married, until you get divorced, until Friday night, until Sunday morning, until you get a new car or home, until your car or home is paid off, until the first or the fifteenth, until spring, until summer, until fall, until winter...
Decide now that there is no better time to be happy, no better time to be thankful."
~ *Author Unknown*

Thank You for:

715. _____

716. _____

717. _____

Thank You 1095
August 28

"If a dog were your teacher these are some of the lessons you might learn: When loved ones come home, always run to greet them. Never pass up the opportunity to go for a joyride; allow the experience of fresh air and the wind in your face to be pure ecstasy. Take naps and stretch before rising. Run, romp and play daily. Thrive on attention and let people reach out and touch you. Stop now and then to simply lie on your back on the grass. When you're happy dance around and wiggle your body with delight. Delight in the simple joys of a long walk. Eat with gusto and enthusiasm. Stop when you've had enough. Be loyal. Never pretend to be something you're not. If what you want lies buried, dig until you find it."
~ *Author Unknown*

Thank You for:

718. _____

719. _____

720. _____

Thank You 1095
August 29

"I love Birthdays! Because we party, and because of the excuse to eat cake, but mostly because we gather together to concentrate solely on one person; we give all our attention to letting someone know that we appreciate them, that we are glad they were born, that we are thankful they exist, that they are important, not because of anything they have done, but simply because they are. A person could soar as it were on wings a long time, on the pleasures of being the center of that kind of attention."
~ *Connie Ruth Christiansen*

"Our birthdays are feathers in the broad wing of time."
~ *Jean Paul Richter, German Romantic Writer, 1763-1825*

Thank You for:

721. _____

722. _____

723. _____

Thank You 1095
August 30

"All things bright and beautiful, all creatures great and small, all things wise and wonderful, the Lord God made them all.

Each little flower that opens, each little bird that sings, He made their glowing colors, He made their tiny wings.

The purple headed mountains, the river running by, the sunset and the morning that brightens up the sky.

The cold wind in the winter, the pleasant summer sun, the ripe fruits in the garden, He made them every one.

The tall trees in the greenwood, the meadows where we play, the rushes by the water, to gather every day.

He gave us eyes to see them, and lips that we might tell how great is God Almighty, who has made all things well."

~ *Cecil Frances Humphreys Alexander, Founder of a school for the deaf, Author of 400 hymns, 1818-1895*

Thank You for:

724. _____

725. _____

726. _____

Thank You 1095
August 31

"Each moment of the year has its own beauty."
~ *Ralph Waldo Emerson, American Poet, Philosopher, 1808-1882*

"We thank You for our senses, by which we hear the songs of birds, and see the splendor of the summer fields and taste of the autumn fruits, and rejoice in the feel of snow, and smell the breath of spring. Grant us a heart wide open to all this beauty; and save our souls from being so blind that we pass unseeing when even the common thornbush is aflame with Your glory."
~ *Walter Rauschenbusch, Theologian, Baptist Minister, Socialist Reformer, Writer, 1861-1918*

Thank You for:

727. _____

728. _____

729. _____

Thank You 1095
September 1

"The adventure of life is to learn. The purpose of life is to grow. The nature of life is to change. The challenge of life is to overcome. The essence of life is to care. The opportunity of life is to serve. The secret of life is to dare. The spice of life is to befriend. The beauty of life is to give. The joy of life is to love."
~ *William A. Ward, one of America's most quoted writers of inspirational maxims, 1921-1994*

"The secret to happiness is to be thankful."
~ *Author Unknown*

Thank You for:

730. _____

731. _____

732. _____

Thank You 1095
September 2

"Have you ever wondered what life would be like without hair? No locks to preen, no eyelashes to curl or eyebrows to pluck, no mustaches or beards to shave or comb, no signature style, no curls or straight, long or short, thick or thin, or thinning, no red, brunette or blonde.

Of course, if God had not given us hair in the first place we would not miss it, but I for one am grateful for it."
~ *Connie Ruth Christiansen*

"And forget not that the earth delights to feel your bare feet and the winds long to play with your hair."
~ *Khalil Gibran, Lebanese American Poet, Author of The Prophet, 1883-1931*

Thank You for:

733. _____

734. _____

735. _____

Thank You 1095
September 3

"What can I be thankful for today? I mused. I will go back in my memory and find something different, something unique to all my other thanks, I decided. It didn't take long until I began to recall all the containers that have come and gone from my life – How different my life would be without all of the containers to put important and not so important things in: drawers for clothing and for paper, and for all the little do-dads that wouldn't have a home otherwise; plastic tubs with lids for food in the fridge; boxes for cereals, pastas, and all the photos I will someday put into an album; packing crates, and ottomans with hidden storage spaces; purses, and pockets, and other places; square, rectangle, round, or oblong, deep or shallow, plain or decorative, I am thankful for containers, and for the people who put them together, ready for the convenience of my life."
~ Connie Ruth Christiansen

Thank You for:

736. _____

737. _____

738. _____

Thank You 1095
September 4

"There is no season such a delight can bring as summer, autumn, winter, and the spring."
~ *William Browne, English Poet, 1590-1625*

"Sunshine is delicious, rain is refreshing, wind braces us up, snow is exhilarating; there is really no such thing as bad weather, only different kinds of good weather."
~ *John Ruskin, English Poet, Artist, Critic, 1819-1900*

"And you would accept the seasons of your heart just as you have always accepted that seasons pass over your fields and you would watch with serenity through the winters of your grief."
~ *Khalil Gibran, Lebanese American Poet, Author of The Prophet, 1883-1931*

Thank You for:

739. _____

740. _____

741. _____

Thank You 1095
September 5

"Learning is a treasure that will follow its owner everywhere."
~ Ancient Chinese Proverb

"Little plaid dresses and white ankle socks, new jeans and tennies, and a yellow pencil box; backpacks and rulers and crisp white lined paper, notebooks and pee-chees, and calculators; anticipation of the first day of school, earlier bedtimes and learning the rules, or depending on your age, Autumn nostalgia like leaves in the wind."
~ Connie Ruth Christiansen

Thank You for:

742. _____

743. _____

744. _____

Thank You 1095
September 6

"A book is like a garden carried in the pocket."
~ *Chinese Proverb*

"A-Z, a group of otherwise meaningless shapes, the creative combination of which, when placed just so on a page can erupt guffaws of laughter or bring tears to the eyes; cause the love-sick heart to ache with desire or soothe the lonely hours of the mourner; lift the imagination to new heights or inspire slumber; start wars or end them. Be thankful for the alphabet; and for the best combination of letters – the written Word of God."
~ *Connie Ruth Christiansen*

"If you can read this, thank a teacher. If you can read this in your national language, thank a soldier."
~ *Author Unknown*

Thank You for:

745. _____

746. _____

747. _____

Thank You 1095
September 7

"There is nothing like returning to a place that remains unchanged to find the ways in which you yourself have altered."
~ *Nelson Mandela, South African Anti-Apartheid Activist, President, Nobel Peace Prize recipient*

"The things which the child loves remain in the domain of the heart until old age. The most beautiful thing in life is that our souls remain over the places where we once enjoyed ourselves."
~ *Khalil Gibran, Lebanese American Artist, Poet, Author of 'The Prophet,' 1883-1931*

"It's never too late to have a happy childhood."
Author Unknown

Thank You for:

748. _____

749. _____

750. _____

Thank You 1095
September 8

"Do not be anxious about anything, but in every situation, by prayer and petition, with thanksgiving, present your requests to God. And the peace of God, which transcends all understanding, will guard your hearts and minds."
~ Philippians 4:6-7 NIV

"A thankful heart may or may not change your circumstances, but it will change you."
~ Author Unknown

Thank You for:

751. _____

752. _____

753. _____

Thank You 1095
September 9

"Water is as the paradox of life. It is the most yielding and flexible of elements, and yet when it comes in force, nothing can stop it."
~ *Ancient Chinese Saying*

"Surely God with all His power could have created this life with no need for water. How different life would be without the cold, the cool, the warm and the hot of this pure, delightfully satisfying liquid. Who can imagine a life with no fish, no boats, no rain, no starfish, no porpoises or whales, no otters or beavers, no wet to dip our feet in, to soak our sore muscles in; no thirsty to be quenched."
~ *Connie Ruth Christiansen*

"If any man thirst, let him come unto Me, and drink."
~ *Invitation from Jesus, John 7:37 NIV*

Thank You for:

754. _____

755. _____

756. _____

Thank You 1095
September 10

"Can you almost smell it; the enticing aroma of fresh baking bread? Just the thought of it can trigger nostalgia; bring taste buds to life.
 Thank You for bread, just out of the oven, just out of the bag, just out of the toaster; for the crunchy of crust and the soft of the center; for sliced bread and breadsticks and muffins and biscuits, and croutons. And thank You for the eternal Bread of Life."
 ~ Connie Ruth Christiansen

"Man does not live by bread alone, but by every word that proceeds out of the mouth of God."
 ~ Deuteronomy 8:3a NASB

Thank You for:

757. _____

758. _____

759. _____

Thank You 1095
September 11

"When someone or something you love becomes a memory, that memory becomes a treasure."
~ *Author Unknown*

"In remembrance of those who were taken from us by men who loved hate more than freedom; for all the brave souls who give time and gave life for liberties taken for granted; for a country that with all of her faults is still the best, the beautiful, the brightest, and the only place I want to call home, I give thanks."
~ *Connie Ruth Christiansen*

Thank You for:

760. _____

761. _____

762. _____

Thank You 1095
September 12

"A story is told of a man and woman who gave a sizeable contribution at their place of worship to honor the memory of their son who lost his life in the war. When the announcement was made of this generous donation, another woman whispered to her husband, "Let's give the same amount in honor of our son." Her husband whispered back, "What are you talking about? Our son wasn't killed, he came home safe." She answered, "That's just the point. Let's honor him by giving a donation as an expression of thanks that he is still with us.""
~ *Author Unknown*

"We often take for granted the very things that most deserve our thanks."
~ *Author Unknown*

Thank You for:

763. _____

764. _____

765. _____

Thank You 1095
September 13

"Be thankful that everywhere we look are clues to life and to our success. For instance, look up and learn lessons from a flock of geese:

As each goose flaps its wings, it creates an up-lift for the birds behind. The V formation adds 70 percent greater flying range than if each bird flew alone. When a goose falls out of formation, it feels the drag and resistance of flying alone. It quickly moves back into formation to take advantage of the lifting power of the birds in front. When the lead goose tires it rotates back into the formation and another goose flies to the point position. Geese honk to encourage those up front to keep up their speed.

When a goose gets sick, wounded, or shot down, two geese often follow it down; stay with it until it dies or flies again. Then they all launch out to catch up to the flock, or to join another formation."
~ Author Unknown

Thank You for:

766. _____

767. _____

768. _____

Thank You 1095
September 14

"Eight Gifts that don't cost a monetary thing, but that have power to bless a person's day; change a person's life:

The Gift of Listening – no interrupting, daydreaming or planning your response;

The Gift of Affection – hugs, kisses, pats on the backs, handshakes and handholds;

The Gift of Laughter – clip a cartoon, share a funny story; laugh at someone's joke;

The Gift of a Written Note – a brief acknowledgement or a complete sonnet;

The Gift of a Compliment –sincere, praise for something they've done, or who they are;

The Gift of a Favor – go out of your way to do something kind;

The Gift of Solitude – be sensitive to other people's needs to sometimes be left alone;

The Gift of a Cheerful Disposition – it's not that difficult to say thank you, or hello."

~ Author Unknown

Thank You for:

769. _____

770. _____

771. _____

Thank You 1095
September 15

"A shipwreck survivor was washed up on an uninhabited island. He prayed feverishly for God to rescue him, and worked hard to build a little hut out of driftwood to protect him from the elements and to store his few possessions. But then one day, after scavenging for food, he arrived home to find his little hut in flames, the smoke rolling up to the sky. He was stunned with grief and anger. "God, how could you do this to me?!" he cried. A few hours later he heard the sound of a ship that was approaching the island to rescue him. "How did you know I was here?" asked the weary man. "We saw your smoke signal," they replied.

Remember this story the next time you feel lost. It may just be that it will be the smoke of your life that will attract your rescue."
~ Author Unknown

Thank You for:

772. _____

773. _____

774. _____

Thank You 1095
September 16

Trust in the Lord with all your heart; and lean not on your own understanding. In all your ways acknowledge Him, and He will make your paths straight."
~ *Proverbs 3:5-6 NIV*

"Think not about your frustrations, but about your unfulfilled potential. Concern yourself not with what you tried and failed in, but with what it is still possible for you to do."
~ *Pope John XXIII, 261st, 1881-1963*

Thank You for:

775. _____

776. _____

777. _____

Thank You 1095
September 17

"Something to ponder and be thankful for: At any given moment, someone, somewhere is thinking of you; wants you to be happy; admires your strength; is proud of you; is celebrating your successes; wants to be your shoulder to cry on; wants to protect you; wants to be forgiven by you; wants to forgive you; wants to share their dreams with you; treasures your spirit; is thankful for your friendship and love; misses your guidance or advice; misses you; can hardly wait to see you; loves you for who you are; loves the way you make them feel; hears a song that reminds them of you; has faith in you; trusts you; is praying for you; you are always on the mind of someone somewhere, God makes sure of that. And when it seems there is no one, you are on the Mind of God."
~ Author Unknown

Thank You for:

778. _____

779. _____

780. _____

Thank You 1095
September 18

"God is love; not just a lover, not just a doer of loving things, not just a symbol of all things love; His entire being IS Love."
~ *Connie Ruth Christiansen; 1 John 4:8*

"Many cars around town sport bumper stickers boasting the achievements of the driver's child: *My Child is a 4.0 Student at Ackerman*, or *My Child is on the Varsity Team at Gladstone.*

My favorite one is: *My Child Is.*

Maybe I like that one best because it reminds me that my Heavenly Father loves me whether I do anything grand for Him or not. He just loves me for who I am. I don't need to earn His love, I don't need to accomplish anything spectacular, I don't need to perform. He loves me just because...I am."
~ *My Child Is, by Linnea Zednik; Used by permission*

Thank You for:

781. _____

782. _____

783. _____

Thank You 1095
September 19

"When you were born, you cried and the world rejoiced. Live your life so that when you die, the world cries and you rejoice."
~ *Author Unknown*

"Past the seeker as he prayed came the crippled and the beggar and the beaten. And seeing them, he cried, "Great God, how is it that a loving creator can see such things and yet do nothing about them?" And God said: "I did do something. I made you.""
~ *Author Unknown*

"I am humbled to be His hands and feet, thankful to have something to give."
~ *Connie Ruth Christiansen*

Thank You for:

784. _____

785. _____

786. _____

Thank You 1095
September 20

"There is one thing about which I shall have no regrets when my life ends. I have savored to the full all the small, daily joys. The bright sunshine on the breakfast table; the smell of the air at dusk; the sound of the clock ticking; the light rains that start gently after midnight; the house when the family comes home; Sunday-evening tea before the fire! I have never missed one moment of beauty, not ever taken it for granted in spring, summer, autumn or winter."
~ *Agnes Sligh Turnbull, American Novelist, Short Story Writer, 1888-1982*

"Gratitude is the fairest blossom which springs from the soul."
~ *Henry Ward Beecher, Clergyman, Social Reformer, Abolitionist, 1813-1887*

Thank You for:

787. _____

788. _____

789. _____

Thank You 1095
September 21

"Four candles burned in the dark, and they were speaking. The first candle said, "I am Peace. These days, nobody wants to keep me lit." Then sadly, the Peace flame was gone. The second candle said, "I am Faith. No one seems to need me." With those unhappy words, the Faith flame flickered and died. The third flame said, "I am Love. No one seems to understand how important I am." And so the Love flame was no more. Only a tiny flicker of Hope was left.

A child entered the dimly lit room and saw that the candles of Faith, Peace, and Love had died, and he began to cry. And then he heard the voice of Hope. "Don't be afraid -- As long as I burn, we can re-light the other flames." The child picked up Hope and set alight Faith, Peace, and Love. And then he asked Hope, "How do I keep this from happening again?" Hope replied, "Never stop believing in Love, never stop being thankful for Peace, never let Hope die.""
~ *Author Unknown*

Thank You for:

790. _____

791. _____

792. _____

Thank You 1095
September 22

"A king offered a prize to the artist who would paint the best picture of peace. Many artists tried, but one stood out from the rest. The picture was of mountains, rugged and bare. Above was an angry sky, from which rain fell and in which lightning played. Down the side of the mountain tumbled a foaming waterfall. Behind the waterfall was a tiny bush growing from a crack in a rock. In the bush a mother bird had built her nest. There, in the midst of the rush of angry water, sat the mother bird, resting calmly on her nest.

When asked about his choice, the king explained: "Peace does not mean you are in a place where there is no noise, trouble, or hard work. True peace is to be in the midst of all those things and still be calm in your heart.""
~ Author Unknown

Thank You for:

793. _____

794. _____

795. _____

Thank You 1095
September 23

"For all *Your* ministries; For morning mist and gently falling dew; For summer rains, for winter ice and snow; For whispering wind and purifying storm; For the reft clouds that show the tender blue; For the forked flash and long tumultuous roll; For mighty rains that wash the dim earth clean; For the sweet promise of the seven-fold bow; For the soft sunshine, and the still calm night; For dimpled laughter of soft summer seas; For latticed splendor of the sea-borne moon; For gleaming sands, and granite-fronted cliffs; For flying spume, and waves that whip the skies; For rushing gale, and for the great glad calm; For Might so mighty, and for Love so true; With equal mind we thank *You* Lord!"
~ *John Oxenham, English Journalist, Novelist, Poet, 1852-1941*

Thank You for:

796. _____

797. _____

798. _____

Thank You 1095
September 24

"I love newly plowed dirt, black soil on brown, in rows, with canals for the water;

I love popping the seed into finger size holes, and covering them over in their own private tombs;

I love the little sprouts when they first appear, every year I'm amazed that it happens;

I love when the garden is lush and green and bursting with vegetable treasures;

I love the taste, the crunch and the fresh of food direct from the earth;

I love the spring, the summer and the autumn of a garden -- Thank You for gardens."
~ *Connie Ruth Christiansen*

"I myself am quite absorbed by the delicate yellow, delicate soft green, delicate violet of a ploughed and weeded piece of soil."
~ *Vincent van Gogh, Dutch Painter, 1853-1890*

Thank You for:

799. _____

800. _____

801. _____

Thank You 1095
September 25

"Live in the present, launch yourself on every wave, find your eternity in each moment."
~ Henry David Thoreau, Author, Poet, Naturalist, Abolitionist, Philosopher, 1817-1862

"One song can spark a moment, one flower can wake the dream; One tree can start a forest, one bird can herald a spring; One smile begins a friendship, one handclasp lifts a soul; One star can guide a ship at sea, one word can frame the goal; One vote can change a nation, one sunbeam lights a room; One step must start each journey, one word must start each prayer; One hope will raise our spirits, one touch can show you care; One voice can speak with wisdom, one heart can know what's true."
~ Author Unknown

Thank You for:

802. _____

803. _____

804. _____

Thank You 1095
September 26

"The joy of the Lord is our strength."
~ *Nehemiah 8:10 KJV*

"It is pleasing to God whenever thou rejoicest or laughest from the bottom of thy heart."
~ *Martin Luther, German Priest who initiated the Protestant Reformation, 1483-1546*

"Joy is a heart full and a mind purified by gratitude."
~ *Marietta McCarty, contemporary Consultant, Author; Used by permission, mariettamccarty.com*

Thank You for:

805. _____

806. _____

807. _____

Thank You 1095
September 27

"Go, sit upon the lofty hill, and turn your eyes around, where waving woods and waters wild do hymn an autumn sound. The summer sun is faint on them, the summer flowers depart. Sit still, as all transformed to stone, except your musing heart."
~ *Elizabeth Barrett Browning, Victorian English Poet; wife of Robert Browning, 1806-1861*

"Every morning lean your arms awhile upon the window-sill of heaven and gaze upon your Lord. Then with that vision in your heart, turn strong to meet the day."
~ *Author Unknown*

Thank You for:

808. _____

809. _____

810. _____

Thank You 1095
September 28

"Be thankful for today, for it is the beginning of always. Today marks the start of a brave new future filled with all your heart and mind can hold."
~ *Author Unknown*

"O, with what freshness, what solemnity and what beauty, is each new day born; as if to say to in-sensate man, "Behold! Thou hast one more chance; Strive for immortal glory!""
~ *Harriet Beecher Stowe, American Abolitionist, Author of 'Uncle Tom's Cabin,' 1811-1896*

"Now is the most interesting time of all."
~ *Author Unknown*

Thank You for:

811. _____

812. _____

813. _____

Thank You 1095
September 29

"To fail at a thing does not mean you are a failure; it just means you have not succeeded yet. Failure doesn't mean there is no accomplishment; it means you have just learned something. To fail does not mean you have been a fool; it means you have been a person of faith. Failure does not mean that you don't have what it takes; it means you were willing to try. Failing does not mean you are inferior; it reminds you that you are not perfect. To fail doesn't mean you have wasted your life; it means you have a reason to start afresh. Failure does not mean you should give up; it gives you a chance to try again. Failing doesn't mean you'll never make it; it means it will take a little longer. To fail doesn't mean God has abandoned you; it means God has a better way for you."
  ~ Author Unknown

Thank You for:

814. _____

815. _____

816. _____

Thank You 1095
September 30

"Instead of kicking the tires of the broken down car, be thankful you have a car with tires to kick, and feet that can kick, and legs that can walk if the car stops altogether. Instead of wishing your long to-do list would come to an end, be thankful you have the body, mind, and ability to go about accomplishing these tasks. Instead of wishing the past was different, be thankful that having any type of past means you were born. Instead of worrying about the uncertainty of the future, be thankful for the possibilities of today.

Stop! Turn your thinking around. Ask yourself: *What if I did not have this thing or that person in my life; what if it was taken away, what if they were gone?* Be thankful for what is, for who is, right now."
~ *Connie Ruth Christiansen*

Thank You for:

817. _____

818. _____

819. _____

Thank You 1095
October 1

"Tribulation brings about perseverance; and perseverance, proven character; and proven character, hope; and hope does not disappoint, because the love of God has been poured out within our hearts."
~ *Romans 5:3b-5 NIV*

"The bad things in life open your eyes to the good things you weren't paying attention to before."
~ *Author Unknown*

Thank You for:

820. _____

821. _____

822. _____

Thank You 1095
October 2

"I heard a bird at break of day sing from the autumn trees; A song so mystical and calm, so full of certainties. No man, I think, could listen long, except upon his knees. Yet this was but a simple bird, alone, among dead trees."
~ *William Alexander Percy, American Writer, Poet, 1885 -1942*

"A moment's insight is sometimes worth a life's experience."
~ *Oliver Wendell Holmes, American Supreme Court Justice, 1841-1935*

Thank You for:

823. _____

824. _____

825. _____

Thank You 1095
October 3

"Life is described in one of four ways – as a journey, a battle, a pilgrimage, or a race.

Select your own metaphors, but the absolute necessity of finishing remains: If life is journey, it must be completed; if life is a battle, it must be finished; if life is a pilgrimage, it must be concluded; if life is a race, it must be won."
~ *Author Unknown*

"Let us run with endurance the race that is set before us; *and* fight the good fight of faith; *for* he who began a good work in you will carry it on to completion; the One who calls you is faithful, and He will do it."
~ *Hebrews 12:2 NIV; 1 Timothy 6:8 KJV; Philippians 1:6 NIV; I Thessalonians 5:24 NIV*

Thank You for:

826. _____

827. _____

828. _____

Thank You 1095
October 4

"We only see a little of the ocean, a few miles distance from the rocky shore. But oh! Out there beyond, beyond the eyes' horizon, there's more, there's more.

We can only see a little of God's loving, a few rich treasures from His mighty store. But oh! Out there far beyond our eyes' horizon, there's more, there's more."
~ *Author Unknown*

"The south wind is driving His splendid cloud-horses through vast fields of blue. The bare woods are singing, the brooks in their courses are bubbling and springing, and dancing and leaping, the violets peeping. I'm glad to be living. Aren't you?"
~ *Gamaliel Bradford, American Biographer, Critic, Dramatist, Poet, 1863-1932*

Thank You for:

829. _____

830. _____

831. _____

Thank You 1095
October 5

"A very wealthy father took his son to country with the purpose of showing him how poor people live. They spent a couple of days and nights on a farm of a poor family. On the return trip the father asked his son what he had learned. The son answered, "I saw that we have one dog and they have four. We have a pool that reaches to the middle of our yard and they have a creek that has no end. We have imported lanterns in our garden, and they have the stars at night. We have a small piece of land to live on, and they have fields that go beyond our sight. We have servants who serve us, but they find joy in serving others. We buy our food, but they grow theirs. We have walls around our property to protect us; they have friends to protect them." The boy's father was speechless. Then his son added, "Thanks, Dad, for showing me how poor we can be, in spite of money.""

~ Author Unknown

Thank You for:

832. _____

833. _____

834. _____

Thank You 1095
October 6

"There are two days in every week that we should not worry about. One is yesterday and the other is tomorrow. We cannot bring back yesterday's sorrows or joys. We have no stake yet in tomorrow, for it is yet unborn.

Today is all we have. Any person can fight the battles of just one day. It is only when we add the burdens of yesterday and tomorrow that we break down. Let us therefore live one day at a time."
~ *Author Unknown*

"I have learned the secret of being content in any and every situation, whether well fed or hungry, whether living in plenty or in want. I can do all this through Him who gives me strength."
~ *Philippians 4:12-13 NIV*

Thank You for:

835. _____

836. _____

837. _____

Thank You 1095
October 7

"Our deepest fear is not that we are inadequate, but that we are powerful beyond measure. It is our light, not our darkness that frightens us most. We ask ourselves: "Who am I to be brilliant, gorgeous, talented, and famous?" Actually, who are you not to be? You are a child of God. Your playing small does not serve the world. There is nothing enlightened about shrinking so that people won't feel insecure around you.

We were born to manifest the glory of God that is within us. And when we let our own light shine, we unconsciously give other people permission to do the same. As we are liberated from our own fear, our presence automatically liberates others."

~ From Nelson Mandela's 1994 South African Presidential Inaugural speech

Thank You for:

838. _____

839. _____

840. _____

Thank You 1095
October 8

"The potter adds dry clay to water and mixes vigorously until smooth. He pours the blend into progressively smaller sieves to strain out even the tiniest of impurities; shaking, tipping and turning the mixture until it is the consistency of his desire.

This newly formed lump sits on a shelf until it is just right for breaking, and kneading and pounding into submission; and then around and around on the wheel it goes, the potter's hands guiding the lump into a useful and beautiful shape.

Off the wheel a design is added, and then the vessel is placed into an oven hot enough to build strength, and to bring out the true colors.

Could it be that what seems to be trouble without end is actually the Master Potter bringing His creative thought of you into being?"
~ *Connie Ruth Christiansen*

Thank You for:

841. _____

842. _____

843. _____

Thank You 1095
October 9

"Nothing would be more tiresome than eating and drinking if God had not made them a pleasure as well as a necessity."
~ *Voltaire, French Enlightenment Writer, 1694-1793*

"Some days the cooking of a meal is as much fun as the eating of it; choosing the colors, the shapes, the textures, mixing it just so, arranging the flavors, breathing in spices and choosing samples for the taste buds at each stage of the journey to the final masterfully sculpted production, presented as a treasure, devoured in a moment."
~ *Connie Ruth Christiansen*

Thank You for:

844. _____

845. _____

846. _____

Thank You 1095
October 10

"Every job is a self-portrait of the person who did it. Create with joy and thanksgiving; Autograph your work with excellence."
~ Author Unknown

"Be thankful that you are an artist. Everyone is an artist. We are made in the image of the ultimate Creative Mind."
~ Connie Ruth Christiansen

"Art is the desire of a man to express himself, to record the reactions of his personality to the world he lives in."
~ Amy Lowell, American Pulitzer Prize winning Poet, 1874-1925

Thank You for:

847. _____

848. _____

849. _____

Thank You 1095
October 11

"A pessimist sees the difficulty in every opportunity; an optimist sees the opportunity in every difficulty."
~ *Winston Churchill, British WWII Politician and Statesman, 1874-1965*

"Optimism does not deny the presence of difficulty or evil, it simply understands that evil and difficulty can be overcome, and can be turned around for good. Pessimism is the belief that evil and difficulty are insurmountable. I see the difficulty, I recognize the evil; I choose optimism, I choose unbeatable faith."
~ *Connie Ruth Christiansen*

"Between the optimist and the pessimist, the difference is droll. The optimist sees the doughnut; the pessimist the hole!"
~ *Oscar Wilde, Irish Poet, Novelist, Dramatist, Critic, 1854-1900*

Thank You for:

850. _____

851. _____

852. _____

Thank You 1095
October 12

"You give but little when you give of your possessions. It is when you give of yourself that you truly give."
~ *Khalil Gibran, Lebanese American Artist, Poet, Author of The Prophet, 1883-1931*

""How can you stand to do that?! Doesn't it break your heart?!" a friend asked when I mentioned that I was volunteering to hold the hospital infants who had been born addicted to drugs; babies that seemingly could not be comforted despite my best efforts. *Break my heart? Yes!* How can I stand it? By believing that Love conquers despair; by thinking not of myself, but of the child in my arms whose heart was broken even before he was born, whose body was battered even before she left what should be the safest place on earth – the womb. I choose to be thankful for those times when my broken heart is the very best and most precious gift I can give."
~ *Connie Ruth Christiansen*

Thank You for:

853. _____

854. _____

855. _____

Thank You 1095
October 13

"My daily survival kit – I take these with me every day:

A Toothpick, to remind me to pick up on the good qualities in everyone, including myself;

A Rubber-band, to remind me to be flexible; things might not always go the way I want, but it can be worked out;

A Band-Aid, to remind me to heal hurt feelings, either mine or someone else's;

An Eraser, to remind me everyone makes mistakes; we learn from our mistakes;

A Mint, to remind me that I am worth a mint to my family; to God;

A Bubble Gum, to remind me to stick with it and I can accomplish anything;

A Pencil, to remind me to list my blessings every day – to be thankful."
~ *Author Unknown*

Thank You for:

856. _____

857. _____

858. _____

Thank You 1095
October 14

"Thank You for Autumn things:

For shorter days and pitch-black-sky nights, the stars shining somehow brighter than in summer;

For foggy mornings, I can't see ahead but I can see my breath, and cold crisp swirly winds that whisper of winter;

For green trees turning to burgundy, yellow gold and blue, for leaves drifting down, carpeting the ground;

For geese fading in from the gray, honking and hollering at me, warning of inclement weather;

For crackling flames on fireplace logs, flickering shadows on the wall and warm on my face."

~ *Connie Ruth Christiansen*

Thank You for:

859. _____

860. _____

861. _____

Thank You 1095
October 15

"Thank You for a the mess to clean up after a party because it means I've been surrounded by friends; Taxes I pay because it means that I'm employed; Clothes that fit a little too snug because it means I have enough to eat; A shadow that watches me work because it means I am out in the sunshine; A lawn that needs mowing, windows that need cleaning and gutters that need fixing because it means I have a home; All the complaining I hear about our government because it means we have freedom of speech; The space I find at the far end of the parking lot because it means I am capable of walking; My heating bill because it means I am warm; The lady behind me in church who sings off key because it means I can hear; The piles of laundry because it means I have clothes to wear; An alarm that goes off in the early morning because it means I am alive."
~ *Author Unknown*

Thank You for:

862. _____

863. _____

864. _____

Thank You 1095
October 16

"Many people who order their lives rightly in all other ways are kept in poverty by their lack of gratitude."
~ *Wallace D. Wattles, Author, 1860-1911*

"If we are not grateful, then no matter how much we have we will not be happy, because we will always want something else or something more."
~ *Brother David Steindl-Rast, Benedictine Monk; Used by permission, www.gratefulness.org*

Thank You for:

865. _____

866. _____

867. _____

Thank You 1095
October 17

"People are often unreasonable, illogical and self-centered. Forgive them anyway.

If you are kind, people may accuse you of selfish, ulterior motives. Be kind anyway.

If you are successful, you will win some false friends and true enemies. Succeed anyway.

If you are honest and frank, they may cheat you, or dislike you. Be forthright anyway.

What you spent years building, they may destroy overnight. Build anyway.

The good you do today, they often will forget tomorrow. Do good anyway.

Give the world the best you have, and it will never be enough. Give your best anyway.

In the final analysis it is between you and God. It was never between you and them anyway."
~ Author Unknown

Thank You for:

868. _____

869. _____

870. _____

Thank You 1095
October 18

"I have dreamed many dreams that never came true. I have seen them vanish at dawn. But I've realized enough of my dreams, thank God, to make me want to dream on.

I've prayed many prayers, when no answers came, though I waited patient and long. But answers came to enough of my prayers to make me keep praying on.

I've trusted many a friend that failed and left me to weep alone. But I've found enough friends true blue to make me keep trusting on.

I've sown many seeds that fell by the way for the birds to feed upon. But I've held enough golden sheaves in my hands to make me keep sowing on.

I've drained the cup of disappointment and pain and gone many days without song. But I've sipped enough nectar from the roses of life to make me want to live on."
~ Author Unknown

Thank You for:

871. _____

872. _____

873. _____

Thank You 1095
October 19

"Little stones make big mountains, little steps can cover miles, little acts of loving-kindness give the world its biggest smiles.

Little words can soothe big troubles, little hugs can dry big tears, little lights dispel the darkness, little memories last for years.

Little dreams can lead to greatness, little victories to successes. It's the little things in life that bring the greatest happiness."
~ *Author Unknown*

"Did I forget to thank You Jesus for all my answered prayers, the little prayers that only matter to me – these little things like broken strings, like finding lost keys and other things? Forgive me Lord...Thank You."
~ *From a song by Ruth I. Christiansen, 85 years, Retired Craftsperson, Salesperson; Used by permission*

Thank You for:

874. _____

875. _____

876. _____

Thank You 1095
October 20

"Today I smiled and said "thank you," and all at once things didn't look so bad. Today I shared with someone else a little bit of hope I had. Today I sang a little song and felt my heart grow light. I walked a happy little mile with not a cloud in sight. Today I worked with what I had and longed for nothing more, and what had seemed like only weeds were flowers at my door. Today I loved a little more and complained a little less. And in the giving of myself I forgot my weariness."
~ Author Unknown

"As a wise householder commands his servants and invites his guests, so must he learn to command his desires and to say, with authority, what thoughts he shall admit into the mansion of his soul."
~ James Allen, British Philosopher, Writer, Poet, 1864-1912

Thank You for:

877. _____

878. _____

879. _____

Thank You 1095
October 21

"Be grateful for the kindly friends that walk along your way; Be grateful for the skies of blue that smile from day to day; Be grateful for the health you own, the work you find to do, for round about you there are men less fortunate than you. Be grateful for the growing trees, the roses soon to bloom, the tenderness of kindly hearts that shared your days of gloom; Be grateful for the morning dew, the grass beneath your feet, the soft caresses of your babies and all their laughter sweet.

Acquire the grateful habit, learn to see how blest you are, how much there is to gladden life, how little life to mar! And what if rain shall fall today and you with grief are sad; Be grateful that you can recall the joys that you have had."
~ *Edgar A. Guest, English-American Poet, Journalist, Radio Host, 1881-1959*

Thank You for:

880. _____

881. _____

882. _____

Thank You 1095
October 22

"I thank Thee, *on this night that I was robbed,* first because I was never robbed before; second, because although they took my purse they did not take my life; third, although they took my all, it was not much; and fourth, because it was I who was robbed and not I who robbed."
~ Matthew Henry, English Bible Commentator, Minister, 1662-1714

"Remember that you have only one soul; that you have only one death to die; that you have only one life... If you remember this, there will be many things about which you care nothing."
~ Mother Teresa, Catholic Nun, Missionary, Nobel Peace Prize winner, 1910-1997

Thank You for:

883. _____

884. _____

885. _____

Thank You 1095
October 23

"I hold your heart inside my heart as an unlocked chest of jewels;

Your every move fascinates me, like a butterfly trapped inside a jar;

I fear the unknown, but I know you will rock my world;

As you grow I become more uncomfortable, as a balloon filling with water;

Through the pain I will set you free; we will explore the world together;

My little friend..."
~ Lisa Hewitt, Artist, Writer, Horsewoman, Pregnant with her first child; Used by permission

Thank You for:

886. _____

887. _____

888. _____

Thank You 1095
October 24

"A house is made of walls and beams; a home is built with love and dreams. Thank You for my home for it seems that my life would be less without it."
~ Author Unknown

"The lights of home they bring us a sense of warmth and peace. They promise untold loveliness, rest, laughter and release. They are like hands that beckon us, like arms that draw us near. The lights of home! They whisper words of comfort and good cheer."
~ Author Unknown

Thank You for:

889. _____

890. _____

891. _____

Thank You 1095
October 25

"Your presence is a present to the world. You are unique; one of a kind. Your life can be what you want it to be. Take the days just one at a time.

Count your blessings not your troubles. You'll make it through whatever comes along. Within you are so many answers. Understand, have courage, be strong.

Realize that it's never too late. Do ordinary things in an extraordinary way. Take the time to wish on a star. And don't ever forget, for even a day how very special you are."
~ *Author Unknown*

"Let us then be up and doing, with a heart for any fate; still achieving, still pursuing, learn to labor and to wait."
~ *Henry Wadsworth Longfellow, American Educator, Poet, 1807-1882*

Thank You for:

892. _____

893. _____

894. _____

Thank You 1095
October 26

"*Have you* fallen? Do not groan and lament; rather be thankful for the opportunity given *you* to rise once more."
~ *Ivan Panin, Russian American Bible Numerologist, 1855-1942*

"Far better is it to dare mighty things, to win glorious triumphs, even though checkered by failure, than to rank with those poor spirits who neither enjoy nor suffer much, because they live in a gray twilight that knows not victory nor defeat."
~ *Theodore Roosevelt, 26th President of the United States, 1858-1919*

"Get down on your knees and thank God you are still on your feet."
~ *Author Unknown*

Thank You for:

895. _____

896. _____

897. _____

Thank You 1095
October 27

"A smile cost nothing, but gives so much. It enriches those who receive it, without making poorer those who give. It takes but a moment, but the memory of it sometimes will last forever. No one is so rich or so mighty that he can get along without it, and none is so poor but that he can be made rich by it. A smile has the power to create happiness in the home, foster goodwill in business, and is the countersign of friendship. It can bring rest to the weary, cheer to the discouraged, sunshine to the sad. And yet, it cannot be bought, begged, borrowed, or stolen, for it is something that is of no value to anyone until it is given away. Some people are too tired to give you a smile. Give them one of yours, as none needs a smile so much as he who has no more to give."
~ *Author Unknown*

"A smile is the lighting system of the face, the cooling system of the head and the heating system of the heart."
~ *Author Unknown*

Thank You for:

898. _____

899. _____

900. _____

Thank You 1095
October 28

"Just being happy is a fine thing to do; looking on the bright side rather than the blue; sad or sunny musing is largely in the choosing, and just being happy is brave work and true."
~Author Unknown

"It seems to me that to be happy is in itself a kind of gratitude."
~ Author Unknown

"Thousands of candles can be lit from a single candle, and the life of the candle will not be shortened. In the same way, happiness never decreases by being shared."
~ Author Unknown

Thank You for:

901. _____

902. _____

903. _____

Thank You 1095
October 29

"If anyone would tell you the shortest, surest way to happiness and all perfection, he must tell you to make it a rule for yourself to thank and praise God for everything that happens to you. For it is certain that whatever seeming calamity happens to you, if you thank and praise God for it, you turn it into a blessing."
~ William Law, British Teacher, Pastor, Author, 1686-1761

"I look at a stone cutter hammering away at his rock, perhaps a hundred times without as much as a crack showing in it; Yet at the hundred-and-first blow it will split in two. And I know it was not the last blow that did it, but all that had gone before."
~ Jacob A. Riis, Social Reformer, documentary Photographer, Journalist, 1849-1914

Thank You for:

904. _____

905. _____

906. _____

Thank You 1095
October 30

"Whatever we need most, is what we most need to give. Do you need encouragement, give encouragement; Do you need love, give love; Do you need hope, give hope; Do you need help, give help; Do you need thanks, give thanks."
~ Author Unknown

"Give and you will receive. Your gift will return to you in full."
~ Luke 6:38 NLT

"If you always think what you've always thought, you will always do what you've always done. If you always do what you've always done, you will always get what you've always got."
~ Author Unknown

Thank You for:

907. _____

908. _____

909. _____

Thank You 1095
October 31

"While working in a hospital I met a little girl named Liz who was suffering from a rare disease. Her only hope was a blood transfusion from her five year old brother Joe. The doctor asked Joe if he would be willing to give his blood to his sister. I saw him hesitate for only a moment before taking a deep breath and saying, "Yes, I'll do it, if it will save her life." As the transfusion progressed, Joe lay in bed next to his sister and smiled, as we all did, watching the color returning to her cheeks. Then his face grew pale and his smile faded, and he asked with a trembling voice, "Will I start to die right away?" Little Joe had misunderstood; he thought that he was going to have to give Liz all of his blood in order to save her. He was willing because of love."
~ Author Unknown

"No greater love has a man than that he lay down his life for a friend."
~ John 15:13 NKJV

Thank You for:

910. _____

911. _____

912. _____

Thank You 1095
November 1

"The mother eagle wrecks the nest to make her fledglings fly, but watches each with wings outstretched, and fierce maternal eye; And swoops if any fail to soar, and lands them on the crag once more. So God at times breaks up our nest, lest, sunk in slothful ease our souls' wings molt and lose the zest for battle with the breeze; but ever waits, with arms of love, to bear our souls all ills above."
~ *William Arthur Dunkerley, English Journalist, Novelist, Poet, 1852-1941*

"The most difficult of trials cannot trump His greatest gift of Love which has the power to transform disappointment and pain by providing a pathway to hope."
~ *Connie Ruth Christiansen*

Thank You for:

913. _____

914. _____

915. _____

Thank You 1095
November 2

"Open your arms and welcome the joy of today!"
~ *Author Unknown*

"Where your pleasure is, there you will find your treasure; Where your treasure is, there you will find your heart; And where your heart is, there you will find your happiness."
~ *Augustine, Bishop and Scholar, 354-430*

"Carpe diem (Sieze the day!)"
~ *From a poem by Greek Poet Horace, 65-8 BC*

Thank You for:

916. _____

917. _____

918. _____

Thank You 1095
November 3

"Write it on your heart that every day is the best day of the year."
  ~ *Ralph Waldo Emerson, American Philosopher, Poet, 1808-1882*

"Live your life while you have it. Life is a splendid gift – there is nothing small about it."
  ~*Florence Nightingale, AKA the Lady with the Lamp, The Founder of Modern Nursing, 1820-1910*

"Oh the wild joys of living! The leaping from rock to rock...the cool silver shock of the plunge in a pool's living waters."
  ~ *Robert Browning, British Poet, Husband of Elizabeth Barrett Browning, 1812-1889*

Thank You for:

919. _____

920. _____

921. _____

Thank You 1095
November 4

"I like that growing older grants you a sense of power; a sense of liberty; that those things you were free to do as a child but somehow lost along the way, come back to you as new delights.

There are the beginning people, the children; I was one of them once. There are the middle people; I am one, but I'm doing my best to grow away from them now. There are the end people; I'm not quite there yet, but I am getting closer, and the closer I get the less I care about what the middle people think. I can jump into a puddle now, if I feel like it, and I really and truly don't care what anyone thinks about me not following the rules of the middle people. The puddle is there, it looks inviting, and so I jump in and get my feet wet. The children giggle, I giggle with them. The middle people frown, and I keep right on smiling, and jumping in, and hoping that they will be as young as me some day."
~ Connie Ruth Christiansen

Thank You for:

922. _____

923. _____

924. _____

Thank You 1095
November 5

"I wish you enough trials to keep you strong, enough happiness to keep you sweet; enough sorrow to keep you human, enough hope to keep you happy; enough failure to keep you humble, enough success to keep you eager; enough friends to give you comfort, enough wealth to meet your needs; enough enthusiasm to look forward, enough faith to banish depression; enough determination to make each day better than yesterday."
~ *Author Unknown*

"Have courage for the great sorrows of life and patience for the small ones; and when you have laboriously accomplished your daily task, go to sleep in peace. God is awake."
~ *Victor Hugo, French Writer, Poet, Human Rights Activist, Statesman, 1802-1885*

Thank You for:

925. _____

926. _____

927. _____

Thank You 1095
November 6

"Sometimes your joy is the source of your strength, and sometimes your strength can be the source of your joy."
~ *Author Unknown*

"I am determined to be cheerful and happy in whatever situation I may find myself. For I have learned that the greater part of our misery or unhappiness is determined not by our circumstance but by our disposition."
~ *Martha Washington, wife of 1st President of the U.S., George Washington, 1731-1802*

"There is nothing better for people than to be happy and to do good while they live."
~ *Ecclesiastes 3:12 NIV*

Thank You for:

928. _____

929. _____

930. _____

Thank You 1095
November 7

"A man is successful who has lived well, laughed often, and loved much, who has gained the respect of the intelligent men and the love of children; who has filled his niche and accomplished his task; who leaves the world better than he found it, whether by an improved poppy, a perfect poem, or a rescued soul; who never lacked appreciation of earth's beauty or failed to express it; who looked for the best in others and gave the best he had."
~ *Robert Louis Stevenson, Author of Dr. Jekyll and Mr. Hyde, and Treasure Island, 1850-1894*

"I have been impressed with the urgency of doing. Knowing is not enough; we must apply. Being willing is not enough; we must do."
~ *Leonardo da Vinci, Italian Renaissance Painter, Sculptor, Architect, Engineer, 1452-1519*

Thank You for:

931. _____

932. _____

933. _____

Thank You 1095
November 8

"Another day is dawning, another day's begun; another day to turn to God and pray "*Your will be done.*" A day to slay doubt's dragon, to know within your soul, that as you give yourself to Him, He will bless and make you whole; A day to live with purpose, a day to show you care, when others turn to you distraught, confused or in despair; A day to share God's blessings in quiet countless ways that touch the heart with hope and joy, and brighten cloudy days; A day for sweet rejoicing, for gratitude and praise, because His love enfolds you both now and all your days."
~ *Author Unknown*

"Trust no future, however pleasant! Let the dead past bury its dead! Act, act in the living Present! Heart within and God overhead."
~ *Henry Wadsworth Longfellow, American Educator, Poet, 1807-1882*

Thank You for:

934. _____

935. _____

936. _____

Thank You 1095
November 9

"Gratitude is a twofold love – love coming to visit us, and love running out to greet a welcome guest."
~ *Henry Van Dyke, American Author, Educator, Clergyman, 1852-1933*

"Thank You for visitors expected and unexpected. Even when they show up at times inconvenient, and I wish they hadn't, I love that they thought about me enough to come."
~ *Connie Ruth Christiansen*

"You must never miss the opportunity to say thank you, to tell people how much they mean to you."
~ *Author Unknown*

Thank You for:

937. _____

938. _____

939. _____

Thank You 1095
November 10

"High winds have taken out the power lines. In a few moments my computer battery will die and I will have to dig out the old-fashioned pen and paper to record my thoughts by candlelight.

The night is falling, the rain is falling, the temperature is falling; the house is growing cold. And quiet. We are all snuggled together under the covers, and here come the cats and dogs to climb into the warm with us.

I am, in this moment overwhelmingly grateful for snuggling, and for giggling, for body warmth and soft beds, and layers of clothing and blankets; and for the sounds of stillness that fill my senses here in this peaceful place.

I begin to doze off... *Click!* The power is back on, the hum of appliances, the warmth of a heater, the silence gone. I won't wake them, just let them snuggle a while longer – stretch out these moments of joy."
~ Connie Ruth Christiansen

Thank You for:

940. _____

941. _____

942. _____

Thank You 1095
November 11

"When you pass through the waters, I will be with you; and when you pass through the rivers, they will not sweep over you. When you walk through the fire, you will not be burned; the flames will not set you ablaze."
~ *Isaiah 43:2 NIV*

"The existence of evil does not eliminate the possibility of God, but the existence of God guarantees the elimination of evil."
~ *Author Unknown*

"The remarkable thing about fearing God is that when you fear God you fear nothing else."
~ *Oswald Chambers, Scottish Minister, Teacher, Author of My Utmost for His Highest, 1874-1917*

Thank You for:

943. _____

944. _____

945. _____

Thank You 1095
November 12

"There is no excellent beauty that hath not some strangeness in the proportion."
~ *Francis Bacon, English Philosopher, Statesman, Scientist, Jurist, Author, 1561-1626*

"Better a diamond with a flaw than a pebble without."
~ *Chinese Proverb*

"Some complain that roses have thorns. I am so very thankful that thorns have roses."
~ *Author Unknown*

Thank You for:

946. _____

947. _____

948. _____

Thank You 1095
November 13

"In this life, there is at least one important work that will not be done unless you alone do it."
~ Author Unknown

"There's a special place in life that needs my humble skill, a certain job I'm meant to do, which no one else can fulfill. There's a special place in life, a goal I must attain; a dream that I must follow because I won't be back again. There's a mark that I must leave, however small it seems; a legacy of love for those who follow after me."
~ Author Unknown

"Use what talents you possess. The woods would be very silent if no birds sang there except those that sang the best."
~ Henry Van Dyke, American Author, Educator, Clergyman, 1852-1933

Thank You for:

949. _____

950. _____

951. _____

Thank You 1095
November 14

"Thank You for time, and for the ways to tell it; the sun and the shadows, the ticking of a clock; the shrill of a school bell, the buzz of a cell phone; for knowing what time to get up and knowing what time to head home, and what time the expected-with-anticipation guest will arrive; for calendars and counting of the days till graduation, until Christmas, until Birthday, until celebration; for nine eventful months until the baby's born, for five long work days until Friday and the weekend; for knowing that a package will arrive on such-and-such a day; for the adventure times of the young, and the wisdom times of age; thank You for time, for its benefits and challenges, and that after this life, time will no longer be heeded."
   ~ *Connie Ruth Christiansen*

Thank You for:

952. _____

953. _____

954. _____

Thank You 1095
November 15

"What I do today is important, because I am exchanging a day of my life for it."
~ Author Unknown

"You will never be sorry if you take the time to: think before you act and think before you speak; listen before you judge and harbor only pure thoughts; forgive your enemies and help a fallen brother; stand by your principles and be candid and frank; close your ears to idle gossip and bridle the sad tendencies of your own slanderous tongue; sympathize with the afflicted and be courteous and kind; notice the good around you and be thankful every day."
~ Author Unknown

Thank You for:

955. _____

956. _____

957. _____

Thank You 1095
November 16

"Funny how a $50 bill looks so big when I take it to the church offering, but so small when I take it to the mall; A wonder it is how long it seems to take doing a good deed for an hour, but how quickly an hour of recreation passes; Interesting how I need two or three weeks advance notice to fit a charitable event into my busy schedule, but can easily adjust at the last moment for other events; How difficult it seems to speak something kind, but how easy it is to repeat gossip; How readily complaints seem to tumble out of my mouth, but how much effort it takes to say thank you.

Funny how when I start with a thank You, my $50 goes further, my time is less restrained, my schedule is more easily managed, and my speech is more pleasant."
~ Author Unknown

Thank You for:

958. _____

959. _____

960. _____

Thank You 1095
November 17

"To be satisfied with a little, is the greatest wisdom, and he that increases his riches increases his cares. But a contented mind is a hidden treasure, and trouble finds it not."
~ *Akhenaton, Egyptian Pharaoh, 1380-1362 BC*

"Learn to be pleased with everything; with wealth so far as it makes us beneficial to others; with poverty for not having much to care for; and with obscurity for being unenvied."
~ *Plutarch, Ancient Greek Biographer, Author, 46-119 A. D.*

Thank You for:

961. _____

962. _____

963. _____

Thank You 1095
November 18

"A woman had locked her keys and cell phone in the car. It was late, the stores had all closed, and there was not a soul on the street. Finding an old rusty coat hanger on the ground, she tried desperately and unsuccessfully to unlock a car door with it. She burst into tears and cried out to God, "Please send me some help!"

Within a few minutes a car pulled up. A very large, dirty, bearded man wearing a skull rag on his head climbed out and walked towards her. Swallowing her fear of this scary looking man, she asked for his help. He opened the door with great ease. "Thank you SO much! You are a very nice man!" She said with great admiration. The man hung his head shamefully, "Lady, I am NOT a nice man! I've been in prison for car theft, and just recently got out." He was surprised when the woman smiled, with tears in her eyes, gave him a big hug and said, "Thank You Lord, for sending me a professional!""

~ *Author Unknown*

Thank You for:

964. _____

965. _____

966. _____

Thank You 1095
November 19

"Miracles of earth are the laws of heaven."
~ *Jean Paul, German Romantic Writer, 1763-1825*

"And He took the seven loaves, and having given thanks, He broke them and gave them to His disciples to set before the people; and they set them before the crowd. And they had a few small fish. And having blessed them, He said that these also should be set before them. And they ate and were satisfied. And they took up the broken pieces left over, seven baskets full. And there were about four thousand people."
~ *Mark 8: 6-9 NIV*

"The whole order of things is as outrageous as any miracle which could presume to violate it."
~ *Gilbert K. Chesterton, British Theologian, Poet, Playwright, Journalist, 1874-1936*

Thank You for:

967. _____

968. _____

969. _____

Thank You 1095
November 20

"The assignment was to draw a seasonal picture of something for which they were thankful. Most of the young students from this deprived neighborhood drew Turkey's and mashed potatoes and things from the table. One frail little boy with sad lonely eyes made a different kind of picture. Douglas drew one image – an empty hand. The teacher leaned down to ask Douglas whose hand he had drawn. "It's yours teacher," he said shyly.

As the teacher looked into the boy's eyes she could see a heart wrenching story that he would never tell. And she could see his thanks for all the times she had said, "Take my hand Douglas, we'll go outside." Or, "let me show you how to hold your pencil." Or, "let's do this together." A lone tear rolled down her cheek as she once again covered his tiny cold hand with her own. Her heart was filled with thanksgiving that she could make a difference for Douglas; that he had made a difference for her."
~ Author Unknown

Thank You for:

970. _____

971. _____

972. _____

Thank You 1095
November 21

"Blessed are those who mourn, for they will be comforted. Blessed are the meek, for they will inherit the earth. Blessed are those who hunger and thirst for righteousness, for they will be satisfied. Blessed are the merciful, for they will be shown mercy. Blessed are the pure in heart, for they will see God. Blessed are the peacemakers, for they shall be called the children of God."
~ *Matthew 5:4-9 NIV*

"Burdens are blessings."
~ *Author Unknown*

Thank You for:

973. _____

974. _____

975. _____

Thank You 1095
November 22

"Gettin' together to smile an' rejoice, an' eatin' an laughin' with folks of your choice; An' kissin the girls an' declarin' that they are growin' more beautiful day after day; Chattin' an braggin' a bit with the men, buildin' the old family circle again; Livin' the wholesome an' old-fashioned cheer, just for awhile at the end of the year. Greetings fly fast as we crowd through the door and under the old roof we gather once more, just as we did when the youngsters were small; Mother's a little bit grayer, that's all. Father's a little bit older, but still ready to romp an' to laugh with a will. Here we are back at the table again tellin' our stories as woman an' men. It's Thanksgiving Day again."
~ *Edgar A. Guest, English-American Poet, Journalist, Radio Host, 1881-1959*

"How good and pleasant it is when God's people live together in unity."
~ *Psalm 133:1 NIV*

Thank You for:

976. _____

977. _____

978. _____

Thank You 1095
November 23

"Thanksgiving Day comes, by statute, once a year; to the honest man it comes as frequently as the heart of gratitude will allow."
~ *Edward Sanford Martin, Essayist, Poet, Journalist, a founder of Life Magazine, 1887-1933*

"Would you know who is the greatest saint in the world? It is not he who prays most or fasts most, it is not he who gives the most alms or is most eminent for temperance, chastity or justice; but it is he who is always thankful to God, who wills everything that God wills, who receives every-thing as an instance of God's goodness and has a heart always ready to praise God for it."
~ *William Law, British Teacher, Pastor, Author, 1686-1761*

Thank You for:

979. _____

980. _____

981. _____

Thank You 1095
November 24

"Sing with the wind, dance with the raindrops, soar with an eagle, float with fluffy clouds;

Twinkle with the stars looking out over creation, pull with the moon the oceans up to me;

Shine with the sun upon the morning mountains, paint with the rainbow colors on a canvas sky;

Sway to and fro with tall grass on the prairie, grow with a flower from a seed;

Bow and rise again with trees in a storm, my friends faith and imagination, and I do all of these."
~ Adapted from Dance with the Raindrops, children's song and story by Connie Ruth Christiansen

Thank You for:

982. _____

983. _____

984. _____

Thank You 1095
November 25

"For the beauty of the earth, for the beauty of the skies; For the love which from our birth over and around us lies; For the beauty of each hour of the day and of the night, hill and vale, and tree and flower, sun and moon and stars of light; For the joy of human love, brother, sister, parent, child, friends on earth, and friends above, pleasures pure and undefiled; For each perfect gift of Thine, to our race so freely given, graces human and divine, flowers of earth and buds of heaven; Lord of all, to Thee we raise this our grateful hymn of praise."
~ From the hymn, For the Beauty of the Earth, by Folliott Piermont, Poet, Teacher, Writer, Hymnist, 1835-1917

Thank You for:

985. _____

986. _____

987. _____

Thank You 1095
November 26

"Every morning I wake up and mechanically pick up the toothpaste, turn on the running water, brush my teeth, wash the sleepy bugs away from my eyes, run a comb through my hair; simple things, but are they simple? Perhaps these are very large things for which to be thankful; showers, soaps, and lotions, face creams, shaving foam and razors, shampoo, conditioners and mirrors, combs, brushes and hair dryers, so many conveniences we daily take for granted. I try to imagine what life would be like without them, I don't really want to know, I'm just so thankful to have them. And the next time I am missing one or more of these great small blessings, I will not complain; I will remember that for a time I had them, and that they are a privilege, not a right."
~ Connie Ruth Christiansen

Thank You for:

988. _____

989. _____

990. _____

Thank You 1095
November 27

"He is rich or poor according to what he is, not according to what he has."
~ *Henry Ward Beecher, Clergyman, Social Reformer, Abolitionist, 1813-1887*

"The Pilgrims made seven times more graves than huts. No Americans have been more impoverished than these who, nevertheless, set aside a day of thanksgiving."
~ *H.U. Westermayer, American 19th Century Writer*

"He who does not thank for little will not thank for much."
~ *Estonian Proverb*

Thank You for:

991. _____

992. _____

993. _____

Thank You 1095
November 28

"There are moments in life when the heart is so full of emotion that if by chance it be shaken, or into its depths like a pebble drops some careless word, it overflows, and its secrets, spilt on the ground like water, can never be gathered together."
~ *Henry Wadsworth Longfellow, American Educator, Poet, 1807-1882*

"I am thankful for the indefinable, elements of life; of emotions beyond understanding, thoughts beyond describing, soul treasures too precious to share with anyone for fear of losing them; and for those very few who long to share them, and who will, even if they do not fully understand, hold them secret in their hearts."
~ *Connie Ruth Christiansen*

Thank You for:

994. _____

995. _____

996. _____

Thank You 1095
November 29

"Therefore I exhort first of all that supplications, prayers, intercessions, and giving of thanks be made for all men, for kings and all who are in authority, that we may lead a quiet and peaceable life in all godliness and reverence."
~ *I Timothy 2:1, 2 KJV*

"Thank You for those who spend their time creating and upholding the laws that govern our land. Thank you for the wise ones, who attempt to govern with truth and with integrity. Thank you for those who I may not always agree with or like their methods, that they challenge me to keep on praying, keep on believing for, and keep on being involved for change."
~ *Connie Ruth Christiansen*

Thank You for:

997. _____

998. _____

999. _____

Thank You 1095
November 30

"Joyful, Joyful we adore Thee, God of glory, Lord of love; Hearts unfold like flowers before Thee, opening to the sun above. Melt the clouds of sin and sadness; drive the dark of doubt away; Giver of immortal gladness, fill us with the light of day!

All Thy works with joy surround Thee earth and heaven reflect Thy rays; stars and angels sing around Thee, center of unbroken praise. Field and forest, vale and mountain, flowery meadow, flashing sea, singing bird and flowing fountain call us to rejoice in Thee."
~ *Words: Henry van Dyke, American Pastor and Professor, 1852-1933. Music: 9th Symphony by Ludwig von Beethoven, 1770-1827*

"My lips will shout for joy when I sing praise to You."
~ *Psalm 71:23 NKJV*

Thank You for:

   1000. _____

   1001. _____

   1002. _____

Thank You 1095
December 1

"A winter garden in an alder swamp, where conies come out to sun and romp, as near a paradise as it can be, and not melt snow or start a dormant tree; It lifts existence on a plane of snow one level higher than the earth below, one level nearer heaven overhead, and last year's berries shining scarlet red."
  ~ *Robert Frost, American Teacher, Lecturer, Poet, Pulitzer Prize winner, 1874-1963*

"The thankful receiver bears a plentiful harvest."
  ~ *William Blake, English Romantic Poet, Painter, 1757-1827*

Thank You for:

1003. _____

1004. _____

1005. _____

Thank You 1095
December 2

"Appreciation is a wonderful thing. It makes what is excellent in others belong to us as well."
~ *Voltaire, French Enlightenment Writer, 1694-1793*

"What we have done for ourselves alone dies with us; what we have done for others and the world remains and is immortal."
~ *Albert Pike, American Lawyer, Journalist, Soldier, 1809-1891*

"Wherever a man turns he can find someone who needs him."
~ *Albert Schweitzer, Franco-German Theologian, Organist, Philosopher, Physician, 1875-1965*

Thank You for:

1006. _____

1007. _____

1008. _____

Thank You 1095
December 3

"Thank You for the times when out of nowhere comes a blessing; for unexpected gifts and checks in the mail; for little notes of encouragement, and hugs at just the right moment; for long lost friends who stop by "just because," and for strangers who offer a smile or a compliment; for the deepest cry of the heart being provided from a surprising source; and for that which I thought sure I did not want, but now I realize was my genuine desire."
~ *Connie Ruth Christiansen*

"Something that has always puzzled me all my life is why, when I am in special need of help, the good deed is usually done by somebody on whom I have no claim. Thank You for that mysterious blessing."
~*Author Unknown*

Thank You for:

1009. _____

1010. _____

1011. _____

Thank You 1095
December 4

"At the Seattle Special Olympics, nine young contestants, all physically or mentally disabled, assembled for the 100-yard dash. At the gun, they all started out, not exactly in a dash, but with a relish to run the race to the finish and win. One little boy stumbled on the asphalt, tumbled over a couple of times, landed on his backside and began to cry. The other eight heard the boy cry. They all turned around and headed back. One girl with Down's syndrome bent down, lifted the crying child up, kissed his cheek and said, "This will make it better." Then all nine children linked arms and together walked across the finish line. The entire stadium stood and applauded.

This true story has been told many times since. Why? Because it reaches to the deepest part of us – that part of us that understands what is truly important – it elicits a joy, a sadness, a grieving and a gratefulness; it's about love."
~ Author Unknown

Thank You for:

1012. _____

1013. _____

1014. _____

Thank You 1095
December 5

"Two friends were walking at noon in Manhattan, amongst honking horns, squealing taxicab tires and the noisy sounds of people. The woman suddenly said, "Listen! I hear a cricket." The man answered, "What? You must be crazy. You can't possibly hear a cricket in all of this noise!" The woman walked across the street towards a large cement planter where some shrubs were growing. Beneath the branches she located a small cricket. "That's incredible!" her friend exclaimed. "You must have superhuman ears!" The woman smiled. "No," she said. "My ears are no different than yours. It all depends on what's important to you. It depends on what you are listening for.""
~ Author Unknown

"Open your eyes and ears and be prepared for the mundane to become miraculous."
~ From The Voice, book by Connie Ruth Christiansen

Thank You for:

1015. _____

1016. _____

1017. _____

Thank You 1095
December 6

"The most prized possession is self-respect. The most satisfying work is to help others. The greatest joy is to give. The greatest gift is hope. The greatest asset is faith. The most beautiful attire is a smile. The most contagious spirit is enthusiasm. The most powerful tool for peace is to forgive. The most powerful weapon for battle is truth. The most power-filled words are "I can." The most powerful force is love. The most powerful channel of communication is prayer. The best open door is thanksgiving. The universal key is faith."
~ *Author Unknown*

"His divine power has given us everything we need for life."
~ *2 Peter 1:3 NIV*

Thank You for:

1018. _____

1019. _____

1020. _____

Thank You 1095
December 7

"I am a believer and not a doubter, a child of the living God; I am filled with the fullness of God, victorious in every situation; I am healed, anointed and delivered, blessed and strong;

The Spirit of God is at work in me; I am a person of purpose, I walk in the spirit of love, goodness, faithfulness, and mercy; Greater is He that is in me than he that is in the world;

No weapon formed against me shall prosper; I dwell in the secret place of the Most High; I am a world overcomer, I have all things through Christ Jesus who strengthens me;

I am who God says I am, I can do what God says I can do, I possess what God says I possess, I am because God says that I am."
~ Author Unknown

Thank You for:

1021. _____

1022. _____

1023. _____

Thank You 1095
December 8

"Amazing Grace that falls soft on me; Amazing Mercy that covers the black, white as the snow of a winter's night, with a light shining on the glimmer. No shadow in You, Your shadow on me; I am white, pure white, soft white.

This reflection of light leads cold to the warm; amazing that I the black can lead someone back to the white. Amazing, Merciful Grace – the black covered is now white light."
~ *Connie Ruth Christiansen*

"From within or from behind, a light shines through us upon things, and makes us aware that we are nothing, but the light is all."
~ *Ralph Waldo Emerson, American Philosopher, Poet, 1808-1882*

Thank You for:

1024. _____

1025. _____

1026. _____

Thank You 1095
December 9

"I am trying to be thankful for unanswered prayer. Some of the greatest gifts are presented to us in the form of unanswered prayer."
~ *Author Unknown*

"God's ways are not like human ways, He wears such strange disguises. He tries us by His long delays and then our faith surprises. While we in unbelief deplore and wonder at His staying, He stands already at the door and interrupts our praying."
~ *Dr. Joshua E. Rankin, American Pastor, Musician, Author, 1704-1764*

"God often gives in one brief moment that which He has for a long time denied."
~*Thomas Kempis, Catholic Monk, 1380-1471*

Thank You for:

1027. _____

1028. _____

1029. _____

Thank You 1095
December 10

"Seasons change, friends move away, and life goes on from day to day. Flowers fade and streams go dry and many times we wonder why. Yet we can always be assured because God tells us in His Word, that unlike changes in the weather, love goes on and lasts forever."
~ *Author Unknown*

"Love is patient, love is kind. It does not envy, it does not boast, it is not proud. It is not rude, it is not self-seeking, it is not easily angered, it keeps no record of wrongs. Love does not delight in evil but rejoices with the truth. It always protects, always trusts, always hopes, always perseveres. Love never fails."
~ *I Corinthians 13:1-8 NIV*

Thank You for:

1030. _____

1031. _____

1032. _____

Thank You 1095
December 11

"In the depth of winter I finally learned that there was in me an invincible summer."
~ *Albert Camus, French-Algerian, Author, Philosopher, Journalist, Winner of a Nobel Prize, 1913-1960*

"I shall grow old, but never lose life's zest, because the road's last turn will be the best."
~ *Ralph Waldo Emerson, American Philosopher, Poet, 1808-1882*

"The harder I work the more I live."
~ *George Bernard Shaw, Irish Play-wright, Equal Rights Activist, Economist, 1856-1950*

Thank You for:

1033. _____

1034. _____

1035. _____

Thank You 1095
December 12

""Mister I want to buy one of your puppies." Something in the little boy's upturned face touched the farmer's heart. "How much do you have to spend?" Grubby little fingers reached into hand-mended overall pockets and pulled out some change. "I've got a whole 39 cents!" The farmer scratched his chin. "That sounds just about right to me. Which one do you want?" The little boy looked each wiggly energetic puppy over carefully and then finally pointed to a tiny quiet puppy that limped awkwardly behind all the others, trying in vain to keep up. "I want that one." He said decisively. "Are you sure son? That puppy will never be able to run and play with you like the others." The little boy reached down and rolled up one leg of his trousers, revealing a leg brace. "I don't run too well myself, and that pup needs someone who understands." With tears in his eyes the farmer gently placed the crippled puppy into the boys upturned arms. "No charge son," he said. "No charge for love.""
~ Author Unknown

Thank You for:

1036. _____

1037. _____

1038. _____

Thank You 1095
December 13

"Thank You for these precious lessons that I have learned along the way:

That the best classrooms in the world are at the feet of an elderly person or in the presence of a child; That you never say no to a gift from a child; That having a child fall asleep in my arms is one of the most peaceful feelings in all the world; That being content is more important than being busy; That being kind is more important than being right; That sometimes all a person needs is a hand to hold and a heart to understand; That I can always pray for someone when I don't have the strength to help them in some other way; That I feel better about myself when I make others feel better about themselves."
~ *Author Unknown*

"Life can only be understood backward, but it must be lived forward."
~ *Soren Kierkegaard, Danish Christian Philosopher, Author, 1813-1855*

Thank You for:

1039. _____

1040. _____

1041. _____

Thank You 1095
December 14

"Each of us has a bank account called time. The balance is enough, but it cannot be accrued; it must be used up as it goes.

The clock is ticking, make the most of each moment of your account;

To realize the value of one year, ask a student who failed a term;

To realize the value of one month, ask a mother who gave birth to a premature baby;

To realize the value of one week, ask the editor of a weekly newspaper;

To realize the value of one minute, ask a person who missed a train;

To realize the value of one second, ask a person who just avoided an accident;

Be thankful for every 24 hours, use them up well, treasure every moment."
~ Author Unknown

Thank You for:

1042. _____

1043. _____

1044. _____

Thank You 1095
December 15

"I am thankful the obstacles ahead of me are never as great as the Power behind me."
~ *Author Unknown*

"The word of the Lord is tried; He is a shield to all who take refuge in Him. For who is God but the Lord? And who is a rock, except our God, the God who girds me with strength. He makes my feet like hinds' feet, and sets me upon my high places."
~ *Psalm 18:30-33 NKJV*

"Although the world is full of suffering, it is also full of overcoming it."
~ *Helen Keller, American Author, Political Activist, Lecturer, blind and deaf from childhood, 1880-1968*

Thank You for:

1045. _____

1046. _____

1047. _____

Thank You 1095
December 16

"Life is like a blanket too short. Pull it up, your toes rebel; yank it down, your shoulders chill. It's ok to pray for an improved blanket, but in the meantime, be thankful for the blanket you have, adjust your perspective, tuck your knees in and enjoy the warm, and rest."
~ *Author Unknown*

"It is probably that in most of us the spiritual life is impoverished and stunted because we give so little place to gratitude. It is more important to thank God for blessings received than to pray for them beforehand."
~ *William Temple, Church of England Priest, 1881-1944*

Thank You for:

1048. _____

1049. _____

1050. _____

Thank You 1095
December 17

"A little girl taking an evening walk with her father looked up at the stars and exclaimed, "Oh, Daddy, if the wrong side of heaven is so beautiful what must the right side be!""
~ Author Unknown

"Think;
Of stepping on shore and finding it Heaven;
Of taking hold of a hand and finding it God's;
Of breathing a new air and finding it celestial air;
Of feeling invigorated and finding it immortality;
Of passing from storm and tempest to calm;
Of waking up, and finding it Home!"
~ Listed as Author Unknown in The Book of Jesus, by Calvin Miller, 1996, other sources reference Robert E. Selle as the Author of this poem

Thank You for:

1051. _____

1052. _____

1053. _____

Thank You 1095
December 18

"Thomas Obadiah Chisolm (1866-1960) had a difficult life. His health was fragile, and he was often confined to bed, unable to work. Between bouts of illness he struggled to put in extra hours at various jobs in order to make ends meet.

Thomas found great comfort in the scriptures, and that God was faithful to be his strength in times of weakness, and to provide his needs. From one of his favorite passages; Lamentations 3:22-23, Thomas wrote a poem that was put to music by his friend William Runyan. The song went primarily unnoticed for many years, until 1945 when George Beverly Shay sang *Great is Thy Faithfulness* at a Billy Graham Crusade.

One song, born from the difficulties of one lonely man's life, became the sound of encouragement for many people, for many years."
~ Connie Ruth Christiansen

Thank You for:

1054. _____

1055. _____

1056. _____

Thank You 1095
December 19

"His compassions never fail. His mercies are new every morning. Great is *His* faithfulness."
~Lamentations 3:22-23 paraphrased

"Summer and Winter and Springtime and Harvest, sun moon and stars in their courses above, join with all nature in manifest witness to Thy great faithfulness, mercy and love.
Great is Thy faithfulness; Great is Thy faithfulness; Morning by morning new mercies I see. All I have needed Thy hand has provided. Great is Thy faithfulness, Lord unto Me."
~ *Thomas Obadiah Chisholm, 1866-1960*

Thank You for:

1057. _____

1058. _____

1059. _____

Thank You 1095
December 20

"Snowflakes are kisses from heaven."
~Author Unknown

"Soft silver, White blanket, Icicles dangling from a frosty window pane;
Strangely still, Delicious cruel cold chill, Gingerbread icing rooftops;
Grey sky, Bright sun, Crunchy walkway, Lace on my tongue;
Circles of fluff packed into spheres, flying through the air;
Marshmallow men, eyes of coal, Grounded angel wings;
Long climb, Slippery hill, Descending, Squealing, Landing."
~ Connie Ruth Christiansen

Thank You for:

1060. _____

1061. _____

1062. _____

Thank You 1095
December 21

"Sun, Fire, Sweater, Robe; Pet, Blanket, Cuddle, Coat; Smile, Shelter, Bathtub, Hope; Encircling arms, Pee-Jays, Love; Thanks for all the things that keep me warm."
   ~ Connie Ruth Christiansen

"The glow of one warm thought is to me worth more than money."
   ~ Thomas Jefferson, 3rd President of the United States, 1743-1826

"One kind word can warm three winter months."
   ~ Author Unknown

Thank You for:

   1063. _____

   1064. _____

   1065. _____

Thank You 1095
December 22

"Usually we anticipated Christmas with excitement, but the year our precious 3 year old son Robbie left us for his eternal home, we hoped for it to pass quickly.

Robbie's 15 month old sister Janna, a tiny 14 pounder with a big heart, kept us going in spite of our pain. Although she couldn't say much, she offered comfort by wrapping her security "Bee" (blanket) around us.

When Janna turned 2, she was delighted to be inducted into her first Sunday School class, where she captured her teacher's heart. We were invited to Christmas dinner, and adopted into their family. Janna had new grandparents, and all of our aching hearts were soothed with love.

Now married, with 3 children of her own, Janna hosts our extended family dinners, where we pass along blessings given to us many Christmases ago, by adopting new and lonely members."

God Sets the Lonely in Families, by Linnea Zednik; Used by permission

Thank You for:

1066. _____

1067. _____

1068. _____

Thank You 1095
December 23

"I love Christmas time; the trees and the baking, the gathering of friends and family, the lights, the wonder on children's faces. I love that I can walk through a shopping mall; a place seemingly devoid of the true meaning of the season, and there, over-head I hear through the din, "Joy to the World, the Lord has come!"

In a world where God is often ignored, Christmas Carols, some centuries old, are still ringing out; reminding the shopper, the over-stressed, the lonely of Love, of Life, of Praise."
~ *Connie Ruth Christiansen*

"God sent his Singers upon the earth with songs of sadness and of mirth, that they might touch the hearts of men, and bring them back to heaven again."
~ *Henry Wadsworth Longfellow, American Educator, Poet, 1807-1882*

Thank You for:

1069. _____

1070. _____

1071. _____

Thank You 1095
December 24

"Some people debate the value of holiday legends and tradition. I choose to be thankful for the many creative ways in which we celebrate His birth, and I find joy in the stories that have been passed down through the years. Perhaps the stories have been altered with time but those changes do not amend the Truth of our reason for celebrating. I especially love the legend of the candy cane; that it was created with a crook to hang on a tree, the shape representing the Great Shepherd's staff, and the first letter in the name of Jesus; the white of the candy representing purity, the red reminding us of the Cross; the minty sweetness of His goodness.

When I hang this crooked confection amongst the twinkling-for-joy lights on the life-representing evergreen tree I am prompted to thankfulness for the gifts of His birth, His life, His death, His resurrection, His Love."
  ~ *Connie Ruth Christiansen*

Thank You for:

1072. _____

1073. _____

1074. _____

Thank You 1095
December 25

"Over the years, listeners and singers alike have noted that the song *I Heard the Bells on Christmas Day* is at once both joyful and mournful. These famous words were written in just such a setting. On Christmas day, 1864, the beloved poet Henry Wadsworth Longfellow (1807-1882) received a telegram message that his son, a soldier in the Civil War, had been wounded. Just two years before, Henry had lost his wife in a fire.

As this devout Christian man sat alone with his grief, on that most joyful of Holy Days, he heard nearby church bells ringing, which prompted him to pen words of hope to challenge his own despair – words that would someday be set to music and become a blessing to millions: "I heard the bells on Christmas day their old familiar Carol play; And wild and sweet, the words repeat, of peace on earth, good will to men.""
~ *Connie Ruth Christiansen*

Thank You for:

1075. _____

1076. _____

1077. _____

Thank You 1095
December 26

"His family emigrated from Russia to the United State when he was five years old. His father died when he was eight. Young Israel began working odd jobs on the street to help the family survive. He had no musical training but he could sing and he taught himself to play the piano. Israel eventually found a job as a singing waiter in a pub. The owner of the pub asked him to write a song. The song was published with Israel's name misprinted as "Irving." That one song opened a door of another musical opportunity, and then another and yet another, until his name was recognized around the world. "Irving" Berlin (1888-1989) wrote and co-wrote the words and music for more than 3,000 songs, along with multiple Broadway musicals. His many songs, including *I'm Dreaming of a White Christmas*, have brought joy to millions."
~ Connie Ruth Christiansen

Thank You for:

1078. _____

1079. _____

1080. _____

Thank You 1095
December 27

"Surely goodness and loving kindness will follow me all the days of my life, and I will dwell in the house of the Lord forever."
~ Psalm 23:6 NASB

"Some days it seems that nothing is good. Hold tight then to the promise that goodness is indeed following behind you and that kindness is there too. Let the truth of this assurance lift you up and give you strength to carry on until you can actually see the good again. If you are finding it difficult to be thankful for what is; try being thankful for what has been, or for what will be."
~ Connie Ruth Christiansen

Thank You for:

1081. _____

1082. _____

1083. _____

Thank You 1095
December 28

"Started with anticipation, ended with reflection, in between with bumps and bruises, ups and downs and highs and lows, the best of me on most days, the worst of me now and then, disappointments and successes, tears and laughter, joy and pain, gaining and losing, coming and going, giving and taking, loving and hating, holding on and letting go, living and dying, asking and thanking, questions and answers, receiving and waiting, a few more wrinkles, a few more gray hairs, just a bit weary, just a bit wiser, letting the past go, ready to take on another new year."
~ Connie Ruth Christiansen

"Thank You for endings, because an ending means something new is about to begin."
~ Author Unknown

Thank You for:

1084. _____

1085. _____

1086. _____

Thank You 1095
December 29

"Time has been transformed, and we have changed; it has advanced and set us in motion; it has unveiled its face, inspiring us with bewilderment and exhilaration."
~ Khalil Gibran, Lebanese American Poet, Author of The Prophet, 1883-1931

"Having come safely through a difficult trial, Love asked Knowledge, "Who helped me?" Knowledge replied, "It was Time." Love questioned, "But why would Time help me?" Knowledge smiled and responded, "Because only Time is capable of understanding how valuable Love is.""
~ Author Unknown

Thank You for:

1087. _____

1088. _____

1089. _____

Thank You 1095
December 30

"Remember the happy, learn from the sad. Hold on to the good, let go of the bad. Count past mercies, celebrate, be glad that a new year awaits us with no mistakes in it, yet."
~ *Connie Ruth Christiansen*

"Gratitude is born in hearts that take time to count past mercies."
~ *Charles Edward Jefferson, American Pastor, Author, 1828-1929*

Thank You for:

1090. _____

1091. _____

1092. _____

Thank You 1095
December 31

""For I know the plans I have for you," declares the Lord, "plans to prosper you and not to harm you, plans to give you hope and a future.""
~ *Jeremiah 29:11 NIV*

"The day is done, the sun has set, yet light still tints the sky; my heart stands still in reverence, for God is passing by."
~ *Ruth Alla Wager, AKA The Emily Dickinson of Almond, www.usgennet.org/usa/ny/town/almond/1911-1951*

Thank You for:

1093. _____

1094. _____

1095. _____

Thank You

For

Taking the Challenge!

To learn more about Bud Books
or about
Inspirational Speaker and Author
Connie Ruth Christiansen,
visit **www.budbooks.org**

www.ingramcontent.com/pod-product-compliance
Lightning Source LLC
Chambersburg PA
CBHW032038090426
42744CB00004B/49